ESSENTIAL LEGAL SKILLS

MARGOT COSTANZO

LEGAL WRITING

SERIES EDITOR JULIE MACFARLANE

Cavendish
Publishing
Limited

First published in Great Britain 1993 by Cavendish Publishing Limited, The Glass House, Wharton Street, London WC1X 9PX

Telephone: +44 (0) 20 7278 8000

Facsimile: +44 (0) 20 7278 8080

E-mail: info@cavendishpublishing.com

Visit our Home Page on http://www.cavendishpublishing.com

© Costanzo, M 1993

First Edition   1993

Reprinted   1994, 1995, 1999

British Library Cataloguing in Publication Data

Costanzo, M
Legal Writing- (Essential Legal Skills Series)
I Title II Series
340.023

ISBN 1 874241 43 0

Cover photograph by Jerome Yeats
Printed and bound in Great Britain

Contents

Editor's Introduction

'The essence of our lawyer's craft lies in skills ...; in practical, effective, persuasive, inventive skills for getting things done ...'

Karl Llewellyn

The appearance of this new series of texts on legal skills reflects the recent shift in emphasis in legal education away from a focus on teaching legal information and towards the teaching and learning of task-related and problem-solving skills.

Legal education in the United Kingdom has undergone significant changes over the past ten years as a result of growing concern, expressed for the most part by the profession, over its adequacy to prepare students for the practice of law. At the same time, many legal educators have voiced fears that concentrating on drilling students in substantive law promotes neither the agility of mind nor the development of judgment skills which provide the basis for continued learning.

Today courses providing clinical experience and instruction in legal skills are increasingly a part of undergraduate law programmes. Both branches of the profession in England and Wales have fundamentally revised the content and format of their qualifying courses to include direct instruction in practical skills. In Scotland, the Diploma in Legal Practice, which emphasises the learning of practical skills, has been in place since 1980/81.

Nonetheless, legal skills education in the United Kingdom is still in its infancy. Much is to be learned from other jurisdictions which have a longer history of the use of practical and experience-based teaching methods, lessons invaluable to UK law teachers many of whom now face the challenge of developing new courses on legal skills. The ready exchange of ideas between skills teachers in the United Kingdom and abroad is an important part of the development process. So too is the generation of 'home-grown' texts and materials designed specifically for legal skills education in undergraduate and professional schools in the United Kingdom.

The introduction of skills teaching into the legal education curriculum has implications not only for what students learn in law school but also for how they learn. Similarly it has implications for the kind of textbooks which will be genuinely useful to students who wish to succeed in these programmes.

This new series of texts seeks to meet this need. Each text leads the reader through a stage-by-stage model of the development of a particular legal skill; from planning, through implementation in a variety of guises, to evaluation of performance. Each contains numerous practical exercises and guides to improve practice. Each draws on a network of theories about effective legal practice and relates theory to practice where that is useful and relevant.

The authors are all skills teachers with many years of practical experience at all levels of legal education. They draw on relevant literature and practice from all over the common law world. However each book is written specifically for students of law and legal practice in the United Kingdom and sets learning in the context of English law and against the backdrop of the Law Society's standards for the new Legal Practice Courses, due to commence in 1993/4.

Each of these texts is designed for use either as a supplement to a legal skills course taught at an undergraduate or professional level, or as a model for the structure and content of the course itself. We recommend the use of these books, therefore, to students and skills teachers alike, and hope that you enjoy them.

Julie Macfarlane
London, Ontario
January 1993

CHAPTER

1 Not Another Book on Writing!

> Bullwinkle: Rocky, watch me pull a rabbit out of my hat.
>
> Rocky: What, again????

Popular North American cartoon Series *Rocky and Bullwinkle*

I feel a bit like Bullwinkle. Bullwinkle is the slightly dim, if loveable, Moose in the North American feature cartoon series *Rocky and Bullwinkle*.

There are many good books on writing; there are fewer books on legal writing. In fact, those that deal with legal writing are surprisingly difficult to find. Although skills training is sometimes treated as a mechanistic exercise - rather like a game of join the dots - I have found that teaching legal writing and drafting has been a challenge and has involved both scholarship and innovation.

1.1 Legal Writing and Legal Thinking

I am interested in legal writing because it is one of the products of legal thinking. Clear thinking in combination with knowledge of the law is actually the service that lawyers provide to an increasingly sceptical public. The sales campaigns of law societies focus on products clients should buy - like wills or property conveyancing or small business advice. Yet these products are now being supplied by people other than lawyers. The profession will not survive unless the public appreciates the skills which underpin the development of these products. After all, it is legal thinking that has simplified the design and execution of products like wills and property conveyancing so that such services can be carried out by people who are not lawyers.

It is no coincidence that the first three of the standards set by The Law Society of England and Wales for the Legal Practice Course involve thinking and reasoning. These state that students should be able to draft documents which:

1   meet the client's goals and accurately carry out the client's instructions

2   accurately address all relevant legal and factual issues

3   identify relevant options.

It is true that legal writing does not always display clarity of thought. Indeed the layman thinks of legal writing in common with cold winter mornings; that is, both foggy and long-winded. Most books on legal writing attack the fog and the wind directly, showing how to cut verbiage and shorten sentences. My experience in teaching has shown me that the semantic sludge and the syntactic twist fall away when the underlying thinking is sorted out.

This book concentrates on the connection points between the writer, the text and the reader. It looks at the point at which the text represents the thoughts of the writer and helps the writer in the conversion process of communicating those thoughts to the reader. Since issues of structure are paramount to ensuring clear and patterned communication, issues of style and vocabulary will be given less emphasis than issues of structure.

This book is not an exposition, scholarly or otherwise, of the criteria for good writing. It is a manual designed to help any legal writer become more skillful and efficient in the process of writing. Manuals distil exposition into action. As a reader of this book, you will need to test yourself out on the examples provided and to apply consciously some of the techniques in your own writing. As a writer, you will know that you have improved when you are aware that your expression is more lucid or that you are achieving the same result with less effort.

Like any manual, the book has been designed for the quick dip as well as the long swim. In order to obtain a benchmark of your own writing skill now, before moving past this Chapter, do the exercise in Appendix A. When you finish the book, you can then turn back to this exercise and re-do it. You might then have a measure of how much you have learned without realising it.

I hope you find the book useful. After a short time using this book I hope that you will be able to echo the words of Martin Luther King Jnr - 'We may not be where we want to be, but we ain't where we was'.

1.2   What this book is about

This series has notionally divided the vast topic of legal writing into two; writing and drafting. **Writing** deals with written products other than formal technical legal documents. Writing includes letters, memorandums, briefs to Counsel, articles, newsletter items, even speeches on legal topics.

1.3   What this book is not about

This book is not about drafting formal legal documents, such as contracts, agreements or pleadings. This topic is reserved to another book in this series (see 'Drafting' by Elmer Doonan). Naturally, many of the rules and principles which apply to writing also apply to drafting. Legal writing is essentially a process of *solving problems* and *proposing options*. Legal drafting is a process of *defining relationships* and *setting out procedures*. Much of legal drafting is about *adapting precedents*; more of legal writing is about *original composition*. The differences in these processes justify separate books.

And writing is a big enough topic for one book.

This book mounts no explicit case for Plain English in general or for any particular version of English usage. I have assumed your acceptance that a writer can be plain without being ordinary. The case for Plain English has been won in intention; there is still a long way to go to convert intention into action. Once thinking and decision-making are clarified, the more elaborate features of legal English naturally fall away.

1.4   How this book is arranged

This Chapter looks at:

- the peculiarities of writing for practice as opposed to law school
- the forms of legal writing, and
- the many audiences for legal writing.

Chapter Two looks at lessons from the art of writing, from the technology of the production process and from the psychology of communication.

Chapter Three suggests techniques to help you think through a problem before you produce a draft.

Chapter Four focuses on managing paragraphs; specifically, when to move to another paragraph, when to join two paragraphs into one and how to organise sentences within a paragraph.

Chapter Five moves to sentences; specifically, how to create a majority of short sentences and how to manage the remaining long sentences well.

Chapter Six recommends classes of words to use and to avoid using.

Chapter Seven looks at possible structures and patterns for argument.

Chapter Eight summarises the whole book into three processes for improving writing; a three week course, a seven step checklist for revision and a structure for outlining, preparing a draft and revising.

1.5   Legal Writing in practice and in law school

Legal writers write to act, not to reflect. In practice the overwhelming purpose of legal writing is action, not information. Legal writers also inform, but it is a staging post on a journey also involving narrating facts, arguing a case, appraising options, assessing application and significance or persuading the reader of certain conclusions.

Essay writing at university does not prepare the graduate for writing in legal practice. The student is writing for someone who knows the topic well. Ambiguity, therefore, may be a friend. The teacher is likely to give the student the benefit of the doubt. The law student is often asked the answer to a fact situation from life merely as a vehicle to demonstrate knowledge of the law. The answer, therefore, does not need to be correct. Since the student need only demonstrate what is known in law, what is to be done in life often does not intrude.

Whether in private practice or in government service, very little legal writing is like writing at law school. In practice legal writing is action-oriented and focused on what the law means for a particular audience. Legal writing in practice requires the author to turn a mass of data about the law into information about what the law means. Even articles for learned journals require a clear expository style shorn of ambiguity and a practical sense of how the legal topic does, should, or might, interact with life.

Most people in the community have lost their sense of reverence for the mystique of the legal word and for the role of the lawyer as oracle and medium. The intelligent person who is not a lawyer sees the law as one more means to an end. The higher the general level of literacy and education in the community, the greater will be the expectation that the non-lawyer should be able to understand the law and its exposition. This requires legal writing which is clear, practical and action-oriented.

1.6   The forms of Legal Writing

Legal writing often takes the form of other business communications, with only minor variations.

1.6.1 Letters generally One of the most frequent forms of communication will be letters. Legal work requires letters of all shapes and sizes, from the complex letter of advice about the law written to a client, to the simple letter to a doctor confirming the fee for a report. Lawyers adopt most of the same letter writing conventions used in general business, but there are a few special features which are considered below.

Since lawyers are paid for their advice, and it is the advice that gives rise to the obligation to exercise due skill and diligence, it is important to maintain the formal distinction between advice, information and instruction, even though these distinctions have become blurred in normal usage. Lawyers *advise* when they give an opinion on the law. They *inform* when they are merely communicating information which is not an opinion on the law. Clients *instruct* when they set out relevant facts and tell the lawyer what they want done.

In some countries, letters from private firms are presented as the advice of the whole firm. The letter will use the first person plural; the 'we' form. As a matter of law it is certainly true that the firm is liable for advice given on its letterhead by someone who has actual or ostensible authority to act on its behalf. This does not mean, however, that letters have to be written as though all the partners were advising, informing and being instructed. It is much harder to avoid pomposity using the 'we' form. After a series of 'we consider', 'we advise' and 'we are instructed', the reader is reminded of quip attributed to Queen Victoria: 'We are not amused'!

Happily this is not the custom in the United Kingdom. The following is a letter from Roger H Butterworth, a partner in the London firm of Simmons & Simmons, which sets out the rules about voice in that firm. It is also a model letter for its tone, its appropriate use of simple but dignified language, and the use of short sentences, short paragraphs and headings.

Ms Margot Costanzo   24th June 1992
4 Hodgson Street
Kew 3101
Australia

Dear Margot,

<u>Writing Style</u>

You have asked for an account of certain aspects of style in letter writing in the firm and for my personal views.

<u>Custom and Practice</u>

Writing style in the firm is dictated by custom and practice, tempered by partners' individual styles and preferences. Trainees also receive an extensive note on drafting, but this covers mainly agreements.

Typically, property and litigation lawyers write letters in the first person plural, often adopting a more formal tone than is necessary. We would advise that this is not a style which generally meets with the approval of the writer of this letter.

Typically a corporate lawyer adopts a less formal style with assistants, just as partners, writing letters in their own name and in the first person singular. I approve of this as I am sure you do too, Margot.

Of course, there are exceptions to this practice. A property lawyer inviting a client to lunch will hopefully adopt the more personal style. Equally, a corporate lawyer drafting a statutory notification will adopt the formal style.

Trainees

The only body of people for whom it can pose difficulties are trainees (formerly called articled clerks), who spend four periods in different departments in the firm. They may be confused initially as to when to use each of the two styles.

Indeed, trainees and junior assistants, even in the corporate department, sometimes adopt a more formal style, and may write letters in the name of the supervising partner, so as not to presume the relationship with the client. Even so, as regards junior assistants, this is the exception rather than the rule. In large transactions even the junior personnel involved built up a rapport with their opposite numbers in commercial companies and merchant banks - indeed that it is to be encouraged.

Our Clients

I have one personal pet hate. Whereas, in the formal style, the letter can refer to "Our clients", in the less formal style, this translates into "My clients". Personally, I do not believe that assistants should presume that they have any clients; all the clients are clients of the firm. Although it is a personal preference, I myself, even as a partner, never refer to "My clients" for the same reason. Furthermore, in the informal style, a letter riddled with references to "Our clients" and "Your clients" is very confusing and it is usually preferable to refer to them by name.

Passive Voice

The passive voice is often associated with the use of the first person plural, whereas the use of the first person singular can more readily lead to use of the active voice.

<u>Informal Style</u>

To my mind, the use of the informal style (first person singular and active voice) is preferable for two reasons:

- clarity of thought and involvement in the transaction; a formal style will lead to ex-cathedra pronouncements of "Our advice" as to "What ought to be done", whereas the less formal style would lead to a thorough analysis of the thing which "I" can do for "You" or which "I" ask "You" to do; and

- public relations - the informal style is more immediately intelligible and appealing to the reader who is being addressed as a human being and not merely as a functionary.

Please do not hesitate to contact me if you have any supplementary questions.

Best wishes,

Yours sincerely,

<u>Roger H. Butterworth</u>

Some business conventions in letter writing might be helpful. If you wish to send a copy of a letter to a person other than the named recipient, it is customary to mark the letter after the closing words ('Yours faithfully' or 'Yours sincerely') with the abbreviation 'cc' and then name the person. If you do not wish the addressee to know that another person is being sent a copy of the letter, then the file copy only is marked. Most printed stationery will have provision for you to insert the file reference for your file and for that of the recipient. These references are essential in a large organisation to make sure that the right person receives your letter.

Central headings specify the subject of the letter. In a litigious matter, you would give the name of the case, always specifying your client's name first. The citation if you are acting for the plaintiff will be, for example, *Smith v Brown*. If you are acting for the defendant, you will cite the matter *Brown* ats *Smith* meaning *Brown* at the suit of *Smith*.

Each work place will have its own conventions about honorifics, salutations, closes, the marking of second and subsequent pages and most will have a house style dealing with setting out. Remember to ask about them. Often the word-processing, administrative and secretarial staff know more about these issues than the lawyers!

1.6.2 Briefs to Counsel Often a solicitor will brief a barrister to give advice to a client on a specified matter, to draw pleadings, to advise on evidence or to appear on the client's behalf in court. The instructions given to the barrister are called 'briefs'.

A brief is meant to be a concise statement of the facts and the law. It should refer to all relevant pleadings, proofs of evidence, correspondence and expert reports. It is helpful to introduce the annexed documents in a numbered list and to arrange the documents in the same order as the list. Counsel will be assisted if you arrange documents in chronological or some other logical order. Ensure that all photocopied documents are legible and complete.

The brief should state clearly for whom you act. Otherwise it is just possible that you might find that the Counsel for your client have prepared the case for the other side. The brief should include a narrative of the facts in chronological order. The narrative should include a cross-reference to relevant documents which should be included and marked for easy reference.

1.6.3 Internal memoranda The larger the firm, the more likely it is that you will be asked to research a question of law for the information of the lawyer charged with advising a client. Internal memoranda are placed on the file. They may be used not only by the lawyer commissioning them, but also by other lawyers who take over the file when that lawyer is away, involved in another matter etc. They might also be included in a library index of research on questions of law accessible by all staff.

That being the case, you should ensure that a memorandum first sets out the question or questions to be answered. It should also repeat the facts you were given and conclusions should be marked prominently.

Each organisation will have its own conventions about how a memorandum is to be sent out. Normally, they look something like this:

MEMORANDUM

From:	Margot Costanzo
To:	Roger H Butterworth
Subject:	Writing Style
Date:	June 25
File no:	

Thank you for your speedy reply to my queries about the firm's writing style.

Since receiving your reply, a couple of other queries have come to mind ... etc.

1.7   How is Legal Writing different from other forms of Business Writing?

Legal writing is different because it is about the law. The law, like medicine or architecture or engineering, has its own concepts, vocabulary and ways of doing things. Lawyers have to become adept at translating how they think about a legal problem into a form accessible to a client or to a person who is not a lawyer. For an example of how this process of translation takes place for a lay person, visit your local computer shop or hardware store. Ask one of the staff to explain to you how a new computer program works or how you should go about completing some minor building works. The less you know about these fields, the more you will find yourself paraphrasing what was said into language and concepts you understand. One of the challenges of legal writing is knowing how to translate legal concepts and vocabulary effectively into terms which can be understood by a non-lawyer.

Second, legal writing is different because lawyers can act only on instructions. Like doctors, they need to explain to the client the various choices available to them in sufficient detail and with sufficient clarity in order that the client can make the necessary decisions and instruct the lawyer what is to be done. Often the lawyer will suggest the instructions that the client could give. While lawyers need to recommend realistically achievable solutions, they should generally stop short of actually making the decision for the client. If a lawyer gets the balance wrong and acts without instructions, the lawyer can be sued.

Third, legal writing is different because the legal effectiveness of a client's intentions and instructions might depend upon the form and content of a lawyer's writing. Law is one of the few professions where what is said is what is done. Unbeknownst to many lay persons, legal effectiveness sometimes requires that archaic language or tortuous lengthy forms be adopted. There are rules constraining legal writing in addition to those of grammar, syntax and style. The Golden Rule - never change your language if your meaning is unchanged - is one such rule.

Mellinkoff (1982) suggests that lawyers feel more constrained than is necessary by the overriding concern for legal effectiveness. His research has shown that lawyers can cut out more archaic language and lengthy expressions than they might have thought. Nevertheless, the legal profession is one of the few in which correctness might be determined by senior members of the profession brought up in a different generation with a narrower sense of the styles appropriate to legal expression. Lawyers often worry, with some justice, that even slight departures from the norm will be held to be ineffective. Legal writing is different because lawyers are one of the few professions who can be sued for what they *say* as well as for what they *do*, many years after the letter has been sent.

Fourth, legal writing is different because so much of it requires the author to weigh arguments - to set out the pros and cons, the arguments for and against - in such a way that a person who is not a lawyer can choose the course of action preferred. This requires special techniques for clarity. Short sentences and small paragraphs, traditional features of a modern business style, may not always be possible.

1.8 Multiple audiences who act

Legal writing is also different because few other pieces of writing have to satisfy so many audiences at once. And everyone in the audience might act upon what the lawyer writes in a slightly different way.

When lawyers write in the course of legal practice, they will have to satisfy many audiences, potentially over many years, with one piece of writing.

The author, the client, the solicitor acting for an adversary, the solicitor acting for a close business associate of the client, the lawyer's colleagues and a judge at some distant time in the future, all might need to do something with the piece of writing.

1.8.1 The author Particularly in the case of a letter of advice, the author will use the first drafts of a letter as part of the process of deciding the questions which needed to be answered and the possible answers. After the letter has been sent, the lawyer will refer back to the letter as a reminder of what was said, thought about and decided. The author will use the letter as a blueprint for action and for checking facts and decisions. What is not clear to him in three days, three months or three years, will cost time and money.

1.8.2 The client The client looks at a piece of legal writing pragmatically. First, does it satisfy his or her immediate expectations? Is the lawyer's answer one that the client hoped for (or dreaded)? Can the client achieve his or her business objectives (or not)? Second, does it tell the client what is to be done, by whom and when? Third, are the recommendations for action affordable in both money and time? The client will want to understand those points on a first reading; the client will also refer back to those points many times.

1.8.3 The other side (adversary) A letter can sometimes be part of an adversarial negotiation process. Such a letter may seek to argue a case or to persuade rather than to inform. That which is inferred or omitted entirely might be just as important as that which is expressed directly.

1.8.4 The other side (co-operator) A letter can sometimes be part of a co-operative negotiating process. It might seek to inform and to persuade. The author has to walk a tight-rope in co-operative negotiations. The lawyer will not wish to prejudice the overall deal which the parties have already agreed upon, yet protection of the client's interest might require minds to be changed on matters of detail.

1.8.5 Colleagues Lawyers are only human; they go on holidays, get sick, have babies and double-up on appointments. In the office context, it is important that any piece of legal writing tells the story to a lawyer who picks up the file at short notice. Authors often omit the obvious because it is known both to them and to the reader. This can mean that a lot of time is wasted by colleagues trying to work out the who, what, how, where, when, and particularly, the why.

1.8.6 The judge The fear of every lawyer is that a letter will become the deciding factor in a case, many years after it was originally composed and sent. If you have kept some writing from your school years, go back and look at it now. Congratulate yourself if you are not embarrassed! This gives you another reason to ensure that a piece of legal writing is an objective and dispassionate exposition of what was researched, advised, instructed, agreed upon or objected to.

1.9   In conclusion and looking forward

Legal writing has more similarities with business writing than differences. It is true that the burden of the multiple audience is something that business does not generally have to grapple with. That said, there are sufficient similarities to ask whether we might be able to adopt some conclusions and techniques devised by people who are not lawyers. There are a surprising number of helpful suggestions to be gleaned from people who are not lawyers, but who have had to grapple with questions of clarifying thinking and writing in their own roles as wordsmiths.

The next Chapter is a short survey of the artists and scientists whose work I have found helpful. The conclusions set out there explain why the book deals with the topics it does and the relative emphasis afforded to each.

1.10   End of chapter references and additional reading

Mellinkoff, D   *Legal Writing: Sense and Nonsense*
(1982)   West Publishing Company

CHAPTER

2 The Art and Science of Writing

Histories make men wise; poets, witty; the mathematics, subtile; natural philosophy, deep; moral, grave; logic and rhetoric, able to contend.

Bacon (1561-1626)

Some condemn Rhetoric as the mother of lies.

Anonymous (1642)

Twenty years after Bacon's death the view prevailed that rhetoric was the art of poisonous persuasion rather than of logical argument. Three hundred and fifty years later, the discipline of rhetoric is one of the sources lawyers can use to clarify thinking and writing.

2.1 Rhetoric is back!

Lindemann (1982, p 35) defines rhetoric as the use of spoken or written language to communicate with an audience. It is the design of a message to persuade, to move, to delight or to teach an audience. Modern rhetoric gives us clues about how to phrase or structure the message to achieve the result we intend.

Rhetoric deals not only with issues of style, but also of grammar and syntax. Rhetoric includes both what the author says and how to say it. Rhetoric has also more recently concerned itself with how the audience understands that message.

Most law students have not studied rhetoric even if they have done a course in legal writing. Professor Reed Dickerson (1977) a legal writing expert, argues that American universities ignore expository writing and that legal writing courses are mostly about legal research which would be best taught in a separate course. He points out that writing is in fact about thinking as well as about choice of language, and that, therefore, writing is eminently suitable for tertiary study.

You should ask yourself what direct teaching you have received in writing at school or at university.

The growth of large law firms has brought skills like writing and drafting back into the classroom. And trainers of lawyers, often lawyers themselves, have had to turn to the rhetoricians to flesh out what lawyers do when they write well (or badly).

2.2   Lessons from history

It is said that those who fail to study the lessons of history are doomed to repeat them. Rhetoric encompasses both the art and the science of writing. Here are some of the lessons I have learned from the history of writing, starting with the art.

2.3   Lessons from the art of writing

2.3.1 Lesson One

The law requires high level communication skills The first lesson that we learn from history is that the legal context is a powerful inducement to improving the message. Corax of Syracuse in 460 BC is credited with the composition of the first written rhetoric to help Sicilian landowners win title to disputed property (Lindemann, 1982).

The classical rhetoricians were Aristotle, Cicero and Quintilian. If you read the recently issued new translation of Aristotle's *The Art of Rhetoric* you will discover that 2000 years ago Aristotle expounded solutions to problems that you might have been grappling with yesterday.

2.3.2 Lesson Two

Communication focuses on the audience Classical rhetoric was largely a spoken art centring on persuasion. Aristotle said that persuasion can lie in the goodwill of the author, the emotion of the audience, or in the logic of the argument. Later commentators say that rhetoric is about the relationship of the author, the audience and the text. With the rise of scientific legal analysis in the 19th century, lawyers sometimes forgot about the audience. Lawyers often focus exclusively on the intentions of the legal thinker and the formal requirements of the legal text.

A consumer-driven economy has brought us back together under the olive tree with Aristotle and Socrates. The needs of the audience are now one of the paramount considerations in evaluating the quality of any text.

2.3.3 Lesson Three

Good communication is assisted by understanding the thinking and writing process What Aristotle defined as rhetoric was an active process which included a decision about style and structure as well as content. This process was facilitated by the concept of topoi or topics. Lindemann (1982) calls these *topics-as-methods-of-enquiry* to distinguish them from topics-as-content.

Edward de Bono's techniques for lateral thinking build on the concept of *topics-as-methods-of-enquiry* (1976). *Vertical* thinking aims to take the thinker direct to the conclusion. *Lateral* thinking does not pre-judge the arrival at any particular conclusion, but suggests that certain kinds of methods of enquiry often lead to a better result.

Recommending that a writer think before writing is a mere exhortation unless some useful thinking techniques can be explored. Some ideas for thinking before writing are presented in Chapter Three.

2.3.4 Lesson Four

Good communication has a predictable external structure Aristotle also dealt with the idea that an argument has a common and repeatable structure; the part that states the case and the part that proves it (ed Lawson-Tancred, 1991). This structure is divided into four parts:

- the introduction
- the outline or narration of the subject-matter
- the proofs *for* and *against* the summary.

Cicero expanded this four part structure into six (Lindemann, 1982):

- the introduction
- the narration setting the background and generating the issue
- the outline of the points to be proven
- the proofs for the argument
- the proofs against the argument
- the conclusion.

The assertion that most communication can be divided into predictable topics ordered in a predictable way has culminated in the Information Mapping approach to the writing of business reports and memoranda. In *Information Mapping*, Robert E Horn (Horn, 1977) has suggested that there are at bottom only 16 forms of business communication, each with a predictable list of issues to be dealt with and an optimum order.

Chapter Seven deals with common structures of legal advice in the patterns of logic, time, structure and values.

2.3.5 Lesson Five

Good communication has a predictable internal structure
Quintilian (Lindemann, 1982) added two more ideas to classical rhetorical theory. First, rhetoric should be concerned with writing as well as speaking. Second, a study of grammar should precede the study of rhetoric. In this sense, grammar is about the mini-structures built by arranging words in a sentence, sentences into paragraphs and paragraphs into a whole to form the overall structure of argument.

The history of grammar in English has waxed and waned between a view of grammar as describing actual usage and a view of grammar as prescribing a body of rules about correct usage. On any view of English grammar, there are some helpful rules about the process of building up the overall structure. Yet we do not seem to associate the process of composition with rules of grammar. Ask most lawyers three rules of grammar which come to mind and they will say

- never split an infinitive
- never begin a sentence with *and* or *but*
- never end a sentence with a preposition.

The last two are no longer regarded as rules, and the first has been heavily qualified (see, for example, Partridge, 1947 and Wood, Flavell and Flavell, 1990). Adherence to these rules does not usually help the reader.

However, one idea per sentence, one topic per paragraph and the grouping of related topics together are also rules of grammar which we often forget. And adherence to those rules helps the reader.

2.3.6 Lesson Six

Questions are preferred to statements in planning writing
During the process of thinking about the problem, assumptions and gaps in information will be more readily identified if the writer adopts an active thinking style. Rhetoricians have recommended the use of heuristics - a series of structured questions to guide thinking - since Aristotle.

Journalists use the heuristic who? what? where? when? and why? to check that they have dealt with all relevant aspects of a news story.

And questions in the text? The reader comes to a business text with questions. The writer assists the reader to locate the information desired, by posing the questions that the reader might have, and then answering them. As soon as a question is asked in a speech, the attention of the audience lifts noticeably - even where it is know that the speaker will answer it!

2.4   Lessons from the science of writing

The technology of the production process and the psychology of thinking and reading also contain some lessons for us.

2.4.1 Lesson One

The appearance of the written product will depend on the technology of the age After the invention of Gutenberg's moveable type, publishers started to produce style manuals which were to change the language.

The excision of the letter 'z' from the English language is as much to do with publishers' desire to reduce the number of letters and to simplify the process of type-setting, as it is to do with notions of correctness in spelling. One might speculate whether the trend to shorter paragraphs and more white space generally is due to the greater availability of paper as opposed to the huge cost of vellum. The bullet point has now joined the comma, the dash and the semi-colon as a means of breaking up the sentence, even though its use is yet to be sanctioned by a fully developed grammar of usage.

In short, sometimes we do things because we can.

Changes to the process have led to changes in style and format. For example, the trend to bold type in headings in legal documents instead of underlining is largely due to the present inability of machines called Optical Character Readers to read text which is underlined. When OCRs get better, we might see a return to underlining.

2.4.2 Lesson Two

The process of writing changes according to the resources of the age The desk-top computer has also led to changes in the composition process. Words used to be expensive. When I was an articled clerk, you wrote the drafts and the secretary prepared the final. Words are now cheap. All firms assume that there will be a number of typewritten drafts for perusal by the author before a final draft appears. One might speculate whether the promise of infinite perfectability (coupled with a general tendency to put off decision-making in writing) has reduced the quality of our writing. We now have the capacity to bury ideas in reams of words.

Word-processing programs for the computer literate also offer programs to assist in the composition process. There is now the capacity to generate a new starting point at random in a list of points (one of de Bono's suggested ways to perceive a problem differently), right through to sophisticated artificial intelligence programs which enable the author to generate a first draft by asking a set of pre-determined questions in the right order. Spell-check and thesaurus capabilities also mean that the onerous process of proof-reading has been simplified.

Greater wealth has provided us with possibility of varying work styles. Many legal offices combine the open plan and the private office. The study of psychological types initiated by Jung eloquently illustrates that some people develop ideas and make decisions by talking and interacting with others; other people need a quiet room by themselves (Jung, 1923). Successful thinkers and writers need to provide themselves with the atmosphere appropriate to their needs.

2.4.3 Lesson Three

The skill of the writer is linked to expertise in the subject-matter Research into experts as problem-solvers in such areas as chess and physics has reached the unsurprising conclusion that one indication of expertise is the superior level of knowledge of the expert by comparison with the novice (Chi, Glaser and Rees, ed Sternberg, 1982).

Related conclusions, however, are a little more unexpected. Experts

- will recognise patterns in the information supplied
- will draw more, and more correct, inferences from the information supplied

- recognise the concepts underlying the given problem more readily
- arrange their knowledge in more complex hierarchies
- have more explicit procedural knowledge about how to go about solving a problem.

In teaching legal writing, therefore, most of the development of the writer will take place away from the classroom. A legal writing course should help the novice to develop the thinking skills which are related to the acquisition of expertise - especially the skill of methods of enquiry already foreshadowed in the art of Aristotle (see para 2.3.3 above).

2.4.4 Lesson Four

The mind is a tool with limitations The ability of the mind to select, classify and store information according to a whole range of criteria is at once a benefit and a limitation to thinking and writing.

As lawyers we are all conscious of the selectiveness of even the most observant eye-witness. Our visual perception is guided not only by what happened, but by what we assume and expect would or should have happened. As writers, we must give ourselves an opportunity to perceive the facts, the problem and the law from different viewpoints.

Kahneman and Tversky (1982) have demonstrated many limitations to common sense. For example, people will assess the subjective probability of an event happening as being high if the event is vivid, dramatic or recent. After a major bushfire, the rate of houses insured for fire will increase dramatically, even for areas not likely to be subject to that particular risk. As legal writers we are often in the position of having to rank possible actions in order of risk or benefit; we often need to discuss this ranking with others to obtain other assessments of probability.

Kahneman and Tversky have also demonstrated that once a person has examined the data surrounding a problem comprehensively, that person might fail to account sufficiently for new and contradictory data. In short, we tend to accept data supporting our decision about an event and to reject data contradicting it. As legal writers, therefore, we should postpone making decisions about the overall direction of the advice until we have given ourselves an opportunity to view it from as many perspectives as possible; this also means that when new data comes to hand, we should go back to the beginning and examine all the questions afresh.

2.4.5 Lesson Five

The mind concentrates best when information is sequenced and patterned appropriately The mind also has an irritating capacity to process several layers of information at once. While you are reading this text, you might also be deciding what to do tonight, noticing that your feet are cold and registering the conversation in the coffee lounge beside you. If the writer expects maximum concentration and understanding from the reader, certain guidelines must be followed.

First, information must be sequenced from the most general information to the most specific from the reader's perspective. Some commentators call this *the pyramid principle* (Minto, 1981). The idea is that the author should begin at the reader's beginning, and at any point further down the text, the author should prepare the reader for the information to follow. This means that beginnings and transitions between the parts of the argument will require particular attention.

Second, we know there are access limitations to information stored in short-term memory. Most people can rarely recall more than 9 pieces of information in one burst. For many people the recall number is more like 7. (This is called the *rule of 7 plus or minus 2* (Miller, 1967).)

Combined with *the pyramid principle*, this means that information should be arranged in hierarchies, always proceeding from the most general to the most specific and that the overall plan of information should be grouped at any level into no more than 9 pieces of information. For example, each Chapter in this book has no more than 9 main headings. Under each sub-heading, there are no more than 9 sub-issues. For each sub-issue there are no more than 9 paragraphs.

Finally, the patterns built up by expert problem-solvers also suggest that the grouping should be explicit for the reader, so that the reader does not try to fit it into a less suitable pattern. Patterns of information can be

*   by time, or chronological order
*   by structure, as determined by the theory of contract, for example
*   by logic, organised either inductively or deductively (Minto, 1981)
*   by value, for example from most to least recommended.

In this book, you will find many examples of patterns of information. For example, in this Chapter, I selected the overall structure of art and science (a structure based on a cliche the reader would know) because that enabled me to group otherwise disparate items. The art is discussed in roughly chronological order. The science is ordered from most concrete to most abstract.

In short, every time you move to a different level, you will need to select the most appropriate pattern.

2.4.6 Lesson Six

Word choice is less important than the pattern of ideas A lot of effort in the Plain English movement has centred on the simplification of legal vocabulary. And with some justice. The use of archaic and rare words in double and triple expressions adds complexity to the expression of legal thought.

There are significant and valid concerns for lawyers seeking to cut out doubles and triples, or to use more modern language. Places like the Law Foundation Centre for Plain Legal Language at Sydney University Law School in Australia are now researching how to cut out some words in multiple expressions like 'last will and testament' or 'right title and interest'. A prudent lawyer cannot simply assume that some of the words are not required for legal effectiveness.

On the whole though, research has shown that shortening sentences, sequencing and patterning ideas appropriately and presenting the words with appropriate white space and headings, are the first priorities (Report of the Law Reform Commission of Victoria,1986). This is also a more realistic aspiration for a trainee lawyer who can apply these principles to his or her legal writing, but is not in a position to re-write the firm's precedents (yet!).

2.4.7 Lesson Seven

A writer who plans helps a reader who scans We know that most business readers regard reading as real work. They read an item looking actively for answers to questions that they have. They will look for clues in the text to inform themselves whether the text is likely to answer questions. The use of headings and sub-headings will aid this process.

Pre-reading is to be encouraged. A reader who does this pre-reading and then goes back to read the whole of the text will also have a greater understanding of the detail of the text and its significance in relation to that the reader knows already.

Business readers (and writers) also use the text as much for reference as for understanding on a first reading. The use of headings aids retrieval.

Some systems of writing recommend a heading for each paragraph. This style is used in computer manuals.

The rule of 7 plus or minus 2 (see para 2.4.5) suggests that a heading every 7 paragraphs is sufficient.

2.5   Learning from these lessons

These thirteen lessons deal both with how to improve thinking and with how to revise a first draft. We all like to feel that we think before we write. The next Chapter will prompt you to think about how you think. The Chapters after that will focus on how to revise your first draft and why.

2.6   End of chapter references and additional reading

Aristotle

*The Art of Rhetoric, transaction,
introduction and notes*
Lawson-Tancred 1991
Penguin Books

Chi, Glaser and Rees
(1982)

*Expertise in Problem Solving, in
Advances in the Psychology of
Human Intelligence*
Volume 1 ed Robert Sternberg
Laurence Erlaum and Associates

De Bono, E
(1976)

Teaching Thinking
Penguin Books

Dickerson, R
(1978)

*Legal Drafting: Writing as Thinking, or,
Talk-back from Your Draft and How to
Exploit it*
Journal of Legal Education
West Publishing Company

Eagleson, R
(1986)

Discussion Paper Number 1
Report of the Law Reform Commission
of Victoria

Horn, R
(1977)

Information Mapping
Information Mapping Inc

Jung, C
(1923)

Psychological Types
Routledge and Kegan Paul

Kahneman, D
and Tversky, A
(1982)

*Judgment Under Uncertainty -
Heuristics and Biases*
Cambridge University Press

Lindemann, E
(1987)

A Rhetoric for Writing Teachers
2nd edition
Oxford University Press

Miller, G   *The Psychology of Communication:*
(1967)   *Seven Essays*
                             Basic Books

Minto, B   *The Pyramid Principle: Logic in Writing*
(1981)   *and Thinking*
                             Minto International Inc

Partridge, E   *Usage and Abusage*
(1947)   1957 edition
                             Penguin Reference Books

Wood, F,   *Correct English Usage*
Flavell, R H,   3rd edition
and Flavell, L M   The Macmillan Press Ltd
(1990)

CHAPTER

3 Connecting Thinking and Writing

The pattern of the thing precedes the thing.

Vladimir Nabokov

My usual method ... is to spend the mornings turning over the text in my mind. Then in the afternoon, between two and five, I call in a secretary and dictate to her. I can do about two thousand words. It took me about ten years to learn.

James Thurber

Thinking is the activity I love best, and writing to me is simply thinking through my fingers.

Isaac Asimov

3.1 Thinking by writing the first draft

What sort of process do you endure to record the written word? Is the process of writing efficient and effective for you? Or do you find it tortuous, exhausting and full of unsatisfactory compromises? Is the product of your writing satisfactory for the reader? Or do you often have to explain what you meant when what you said is not clear to the reader?

You will want the process and the product to be efficient and effective for you and for your readers. If you are finding the process of writing essays, letters of advice, briefs to Counsel or memos on the law, tortuous for both you and your readers, then it might be that you spend too much time writing and not enough time thinking.

The stops, the staging posts and the vehicles used in the journey of writing will be different for each author. Nabokov observes that he needs an overall outline before he can write any of the detail. Thurber prefers to separate the processes of thinking and writing. Asimov feels that he thinks best while actually writing.

Most lawyers think that thinking about legal problems is real work. Making decisions about what a client should do is especially hard work. But the culture of many legal work places suggests that thinking is only real work when it is connected to the activity of attempting to produce the final product. Any activity preliminary to the production of the first full draft of a written product might not be seen as real work. Hide all those pads full of doodling and untidy notes!

For most people, though, the premature production of a draft of advice will confuse the thinker rather than clarify the thought.

3.2   Arguments against producing the first draft prematurely

The first draft adds layers of semantic and syntactic complexity to the already complex task of thinking. The author then has to make decisions about the ideas, the words and the ordering of ideas and words. Tinkering with a premature first draft is a bit like trying to build a Rolls Royce out of a Volkswagen. In theory, possible, but in practice, a good result is unlikely.

A premature first draft will spawn a lot of further drafts. Each draft costs time and consumes paper. Both from the perspective of the paying clients and the green lobby, it would seem sensible for each author to adopt effective thinking and decision-making processes in order that major decisions about ideas, words and order are made *before* the first draft. In this book, I recommend that a work be outlined before a first draft is produced. An outline consists of a statement of the problem, the solution and the sections and topics which explain the path from the problem to the solution in the order in which they will appear in the text. Chapter Eight deals with how to produce an outline.

If thinking is done first, before producing a draft, the author can concentrate the process of revision on whether the draft clearly communicates the ideas to the particular reader and wider audience (see Chapter One); rather than using the draft to work out ideas and words on an exploratory level.

However, it is true that some people do not know what they think until they can see what they have written. They can only make decisions by starting to produce the final product. Such authors cannot think through the problem by just jotting down headings for topics and sub-topics. For these people, there is a compromise - the thinking draft.

3.3 A compromise - the thinking draft

If you are one of the people who need to see what they say in order to know what they think, you might have to produce what I will call here *a thinking draft* first. It is called *a thinking draft* because it is used to help sort out the thoughts of the writer. Normally, it would be more efficient to tear up a thinking draft and to re-write or re-dictate the first draft than to try to edit it. Normally, the thinking draft would be used as a basis for preparing an outline from which a true first draft can be prepared.

Whether you prepare a thinking draft or not, some structured thinking, including decision-making, before you write your first draft will save time and improve quality.

3.4 Thinking before producing any draft

3.4.1 Being analytical about thinking

Lawyers see themselves and are seen by others in the community as highly analytical thinkers. Yet we are not analytical about the process of thinking itself. One law teacher once described to me the process of thinking like a lawyer as a bit like riding a bike; you can only learn it by doing it. That teacher was content with a process where thinking was learned intuitively, not taught analytically.

De Bono has made many analyses of different kinds of thinking. In his book *Teaching Thinking* (de Bono, 1976) he describes law school thinking as the sort of thinking that deals with knowledge and analysis. He describes this as *critical scholarly thinking*. But in life we need to solve problems in ways which are practical and constructive. He describes this as *generative thinking*. This transition from *scholarly* to *generative thinking* is one of the hardest transitions to be made in moving from learning law to its practice.

Another writer who presents a holistic and conceptual model about the process of thinking is Ned Herrmann (1989). Based on the work of the Nobel prize winning doctor, Dr Roger Sperry, and Paul McLean of the National Institutes of Health, Herrman has devised a model of the brain which locates four major thinking styles in the brain's four major thinking structures. Herrmann postulates that the more we can use all four thinking styles situationally and effectively, the more competent we will be in our work.

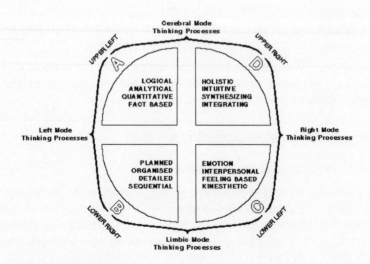

(Herrmann, 1989)

Whilst we know that the human brain is organised into four distinct thinking structures, the particular thinking functions may not always be located with physiological precision as the diagram of the metaphoric model suggests. It is not necessary to debate in which part of the brain these thinking skills are located in any individual. It is enough for our purposes that these four broad categories of thinking style exist. The significant point is that if we can consciously adopt thinking behaviours from each of the four hemispheres before we write, we will become better writers. Specifically, we will be better equipped to

- identify more facts

- perceive more versions of the facts

- understand the viewpoint of our client and of the other parties involved

- work out arguments to persuade the other side

- construct a sequence of events from the past

- generate a series of possible actions for the future

- analyse how the law might apply

- decide how to act.

What are thinking behaviours characteristic of the four quadrants? Examples are given below. Try marking the text with the ones that you commonly engage in and compare your list with that of someone else.

3.4.2 Specific thinking activities

Upper Left Quadrant: Logical and Analytical Thinking

- Defining the problem

- Listing the client's objectives and those of the other side and ranking them

- Identifying the legal categories as suggested by the facts

- Identifying assumptions in your case or that of the other side

- Listing provable facts
- Listing factors for and against before making a decision
- Determining a logical basis on which to decide between competing choices

Lower Left Quadrant: Planned and Sequential Thinking

- Putting a list of the facts into chronological order
- Working out the procedures to be followed in order to carry out a recommendation
- Determining the order for research and consideration of the legal questions

Upper Right Quadrant: Intuitive and Holistic Thinking

- Seeing a relevant analogy in another problem solved recently
- Reaching the conclusion by a flash of insight
- Recognising that the problem moves across many legal categories and specialisms
- Being able to rehearse a negotiation in your mind by seeing the other side and imagining how they will respond to your proposals
- Picturing the sequence of facts in issue like a movie playing in your mind
- Deciding that the problem is a test case which could change the law

Lower Right Quadrant: Emotional and Interpersonal Thinking

- Becoming angry or personally involved about the behaviour of the other side
- Understanding the motivations and values of your client, the other side and the other solicitor
- Selecting language which the person to be convinced finds persuasive
- Sequencing information from the perspective of another person (the reader)

You will probably have quite a lot of ticks next to items which are analytical and sequenced. You might have fewer ticks against the items which are holistic and interpersonal.

The **upper right** holistic big-picture skills are those that we use in devising a new concept for how a legal problem might be solved in a better, more cost-efficient or effective way. Sometimes they involve a future orientation. A few examples might help.

Consider the transition from the original system of proving title to a system of registration. Before the development of a registration system, the lawyer needed to chase a trail of documents back to a good root of title. Whether the trail was unbroken and whether the title was a good root were inferences to be wrought from perusal of the documents. In the modern system where legal title derives from registration, any person can tell by looking at the name on the title who is the legal owner of the land. Or, consider the inclusion of arbitration and mediation as dispute resolution mechanisms in addition to litigation. Both are examples of systems design requiring right brain skill.

Lawyers tend to react to the need for change only when the complaints are long and loud. Thus, the registrations system for proving title was adopted only after many examples of title fraud, particularly in the colonies. Arbitration has long been used by lawyers but other methods of dispute resolution have usually developed in response to demand by clients for something better than the court process.

Holistic **upper right** thinking also involves an ability to picture things. Lawyers use visual imagination to rehearse negotiations and cross-examination more than they might care to admit. Visual imagination is also very useful in reconstructing an accident or what happened at the scene of a crime in order to find omissions or distortions in the narrative as reported. If you find yourself re-designing the law rather than just applying it, you might find that you have a preference for this kind of thinking.

The interpersonal **lower right** quadrant skills include the skill of feeling as the other person might feel. Thus in the example of a rehearsal of a negotiation played through in the mind, the thinker would think through and feel some of the responses of first one side and then the other. Once you can relate to how another person might feel and respond in a given situation, it is much easier to be persuasive. It is also easier to assess the credibility of a story, because you can perceive where a witness, perhaps unconsciously, might have allowed gaps or distortions in the story.

If you find yourself frustrated by the human factor in some areas of legal practice and therefore more attracted to work which requires fewer interpersonal dealings, it may be that you actively avoid this kind of thinking.

The **upper left** analytical style needs no introduction to people who have chosen to study law. The **lower left** organising, sequencing style comes into its own in business. It may be enough to muddle through (or, with a good memory, triumph!) at university without having to plan time or to organise notes. In business the ability to plan time and to organise pieces of paper take on a real significance.

Naturally these four categories of thinking skill overlap. We tend to choose activities which involve the kinds of thinking style we prefer. We become better and better at that kind of thinking. We avoid activities which require the kind of thinking we dislike. What we do not practise cannot be improved. It is possible to be strong in any combination of the four thinking styles. A highly analytical, tidy thinker can have a messy desk (weak on lower left organisation skills). A criminal lawyer with a fine grasp of technical detail may also be good at summarising the case simply and persuasively for the jury (skill in analytical, holistic and interpersonal styles.) A sole practitioner, founder of a large law firm, might not be the best managing partner of the practice he built (poor skill in lower left organisation or lower right interpersonal styles). The significant point is that the best thinkers use all four thinking styles.

3.5 Four objectives for thinking

Thinking has four major processes, which relate to four major objectives.

- **Perception** You think in order to perceive facts, values and aims.

- **Analysis** You think in order to analyse and apply how the facts, values and aims relate to the law.

- **Generation of options** You think in order to generate choices about how a problem could be solved or an aim realised.

- **Decision-making** You think in order to decide what could or should be done.

These objectives are more or less in time order. You need to perceive facts before being able to fully analyse how the law might apply. Only then can you generate possible options and only after that can you make decisions.

Unfortunately, thinking is not a linear process. While you are focusing on the facts, various options will just pop into your mind unbidden. While you are trying to analyse the law, you will experience a settled conviction about the only possible course of action for the client to follow. These activities follow a time *spiral*, rather than a time *line*. You might need to move between each several times, focusing on each of these activities in turn, before you have completed your thinking satisfactorily.

To achieve any of these four objectives you might use any or all of the four types of thinking processes - perception, analysis, generation of options and decision-making - and sometimes you may use all four at once. Consciously focusing on your objective will aid your concentration and enable you to build your thinking skill.

What follows is a list of thinking activities which will help you to prepare an outline for writing. These are the thinking activities which in my experience lawyers find most helpful. Try one or two different techniques each time you need to think about a new legal problem.

3.6   Specific ways to achieve these objectives by thinking

3.6.1 First, start any way you can

Each of us needs to find our own starting point for a particular writing project. I like to scrawl down points around the topic and I continue to re-arrange them in a more appropriate sequence until I have found a beginning point and an overall order. I need to make notes in my own handwriting, although all drafts are prepared on the word-processor direct. At some point I find it helpful to discuss an outline with a few other people. Quite often I start writing in what turns out to be the middle of the work. When I have discovered the beginning, I sometimes cannot use what I have written; sometimes I can. It is useful for me to be working on several things at once. When I get 'stuck' on one, I can move to the next. Each project gives me ideas about the others.

You will discover your own way of starting and the only rule is - do. Work put off until the last minute and produced under great pressure deprives the author of the opportunity to get that magic flash of insight which comes from mulling something over for a few days. The more pressed your mind is for an answer, the further away the answer might be.

3.6.2 Second, start with the facts

Lawyers have a habit of formulating the questions to be answered in terms of abstract principles from law, rather than in terms of concrete client objectives from life. Curiosity about the detailed facts in your client's case will stand you in good stead. The more concrete your statement of the facts, the more ideas you will have about what could be argued or done. An example from case law illustrates this point.

The legal principle from the case of *Grant v Australian Knitting Mills Ltd & Ors* [1936] AC 85 reads

'Held that those facts established a duty to take care as between the manufacturers and the appellant for the breach of which the manufacturers were liable in tort.

Principle of *Donoghue v Stevenson* [1932] AC 562 applied.

That principle can be applied only where the defect is hidden and unknown to the customer or consumer.

The liability in tort was independent of any question of contract.'

The facts explain the principle a little more. They are set out in the headnote as follows

'The appellant, who contracted dermatitis of an external origin as a result of wearing a woollen garment which, when purchased from the retailers, was in a defective condition owing to the presence of excess sulphites which, when it was found, had been negligently left it in the process of manufacture, claimed damages against both retailers and manufacturers:-

...

The presence of the deleterious chemical in the garment was a hidden and latent defect, and could not be detected by any examination that could reasonably be made; nothing happened between the making of the garment and its being worn to change its condition; and the garment was made by the manufacturers for the purpose of being worn exactly as it was worn in fact by the appellant ...'

The case takes on much more colour and interest, and offers more possibilities for following or distinguishing it, if the facts are brought to life. What follows are six techniques to bring facts to life illustrated by an examination of this case.

Be concrete and human All fact situations will have a human dimension. The human dimension will raise questions which might place the applicability of the case in doubt or ensure that it is applied. The human dimension will highlight gaps, distortions or oversights in the story. The woollen undergarments in this case were two pairs of long underwear. The dermatitis was suffered around the ankles. The appellant was a medical practitioner whose evidence was given much credence at every stage in the suit.

(Would another kind of plaintiff have been given so much credence
for what seemed a minor skin complaint?) The appellant had not
washed the underwear before putting it on. (In another era would
this be contributory negligence?) The underwear was not in the
original manufacturer's pack, but had been unpacked by the
retailer. (In another case, could this tampering with the packaging
be used to exculpate the manufacturer?)

Develop a chronology In litigious questions, the chronology
of events will always be important. The chronology in this case
raises other questions for the modern reader:

> ... The underwear ... was bought by the appellant ... on
> June 3, 1991 ... The appellant put on one suit on the
> morning of Sunday, June 28, 1931; by the evening of that
> day he felt itching on the ankles but no objective symptoms
> appeared until the next day, when a redness appeared on
> each ankle in front over an area of about 2 1/2 inches by
> 1 1/2 inches. The appellant treated himself with calomile
> lotion, but the irritation was such that he scratched the
> places till he bled. On Sunday, July 5, he changed his
> underwear and put on the other set which he had purchased
> from the retailers; ... he changed again on July 12. Though
> his skin trouble was getting worse, he did not attribute it to
> the underwear, but on July 13 he consulted a dermatologist,
> Dr Upton, who advised him to discard the underwear ...

This chronology reveals that Dr Grant only changed his
underwear weekly. In 1931, this was the sober habit of Christian
gentlemen; one bathed on Saturday evening and put on clean
underwear ready to go clean to church on Sunday morning. The
chronology also reveals that Dr Grant treated himself. It was more
than a fortnight before he bothered to consult a colleague who
diagnosed the causal connection between the dermatitis and the
suspect underwear immediately.

Add a dash of cinema Where the success of a case requires
a reconstruction of events, it is often helpful to try to visualise
what must have happened, rather like a picture being played
through frame by frame. You have probably used this technique

when you misplace your car keys at home, retracing every move from the time you entered the house last, what you were carrying at the time, and so on.

Try for a view In all fact situations which involve concrete objects and places, it is desirable to inspect. In cases involving locations, you should also prepare a rough plan with measurements to give you something to focus your thoughts on, to help you understand the situation better and to identify gaps in your client's case or that of the other side.

Prepare a diagram of relationships Many fact situations involving the actions of a mixture of companies, trusts and natural persons take a half a page or so to explain in chronological order. This can take a couple of minutes to read. Yet a diagram of the relationships and relevant events will take up less space and takes much less time to read. For people with visual memories, the diagram will recall many of the facts, events and relationships in a way that text does not.

Ask who, what, where, when, why (and how) A good starting point is for the thinker to ask these five simple questions about the subject-mattter to focus thinking.

Practise using them to identify possible gaps in the facts as stated in the headnote from *Grant v Australian Knitting Mills* already quoted.

3.6.3 Third, focus on action and objectives

Say what is to be done Too often we think about legal problems only in abstract legal terms. For example, we think about advice being 'the choice of business structure for a client wishing to purchase a retail outlet'.

From the client's perspective, such advice is actually more often about whether the client should stop operating in the present way - maybe as sole trader or in partnership - and whether a change is warranted.

In a negligence case, a lawyer might characterise the case as a matter of satisfying the onus of proof that there was negligence and reliance, whereas a client will think about the case in terms of whether sufficient compensation will be awarded to cover medical expenses, pain and suffering and consequential loss.

When preparing any text, one of the first things you need to decide is what you, the client or other readers want or need to do with the information. You might reserve recommendations about what should or could be done until the end. In a brief to Counsel, a statement of what you want Counsel to do will generally appear first.

Objectives bring objectivity In litigious questions, the cost of litigation and the amount of management time likely to be consumed by the client often come as a rude shock. You need to think about what the client is seeking to achieve in coming to you. Clients rarely want to pay what it costs only to enforce a legal principle. You should know what the client thinks would be a good and a bad result and the minimum you are expected to achieve.

In giving commercial advice you need to know what the client seeks to achieve, by when and at what cost. Does the client really expect to get out of the watertight lease or would a reduction in rent be satisfactory? Does the client really want you to negotiate aggressively over every aspect of the computer supply agreement, or is it more important to focus on the big issues and to ensure that the client can sign the agreement in time to receive the tax concession available only for this fiscal year?

It is also worthwhile thinking about the other side's objectives. Does the insurance company really think that it can escape liability here, or does it always contest claims until the door of the court, on the basis that some people get discouraged and withdraw their claim or settle for very little?

3.6.4 Fourth, define the legal problem

Unless we control the use of language, we can lose simple ideas through the fog of complex language. It is helpful for thinking to reduce the question to as few words as possible and to use simple words. You should settle upon the key concepts and relevant descriptive words before preparing even a thinking draft.

The Golden Rule One useful principle for writing and drafting is known as The Golden Rule. The Golden Rule requires that you retain the same language where the ideas have not changed. Conversely, where you want to express a slightly different idea, try to use a different word.

This principle has been adopted as a recommended procedure in other disciplines. One style of writing recommended for the production of computer manuals called Information Mapping (Horn, 1977) (see Chapter Two, para 2.3.4) recommends consistent use of language as one of its key principles.

Start with the names of the parties. If the parties are companies with long names, adopt a short descriptive abbreviation for them. Therefore, in an advice about the Bank of Commerce and Credit and the Inland Revenue Commissioner, you might use the abbreviations 'BCCI' and 'IRC'.

If you are preparing an advice on the enforceability of a sales agreement, decide whether you will call the parties *buyer* and *seller* or *vendor* and *purchaser*. If you are advising about the terms of an employment agreement you are yet to draft, decide before you prepare the first draft of the advice whether you will refer to the parties as *employer* and *employee*, or by name. Remember, be consistent.

The Golden Rule also applies when describing the relevant legal principles which apply to the facts of the client's case. Case law is notorious for throwing up alternative formulations of words which refer to the same idea. For example, where a company gives a guarantee for a related company there is case law to the effect that the guarantor must have received some *consideration*, *material benefit* or *tangible benefit* in order for the guarantee to be enforceable against it. The three expressions seem to be used interchangeably. You might need to use all three in argument to the court or to the other side, but in explaining the law to the client, it is less confusing for you both if you choose one of the expressions consistently throughout the advice.

When advising on the terms of a document already in existence, it is be sensible to adopt the language of the document itself. Likewise when discussing the language of a statute, it is sensible to use the language of the statute, even if you need to abbreviate it somewhat.

Label the legal arguments. It is also helpful if you label points to reflect their status in the argument. Order legal arguments so that you set out the rule or principle, then give supporting examples and then follow with exceptions or qualifications. Rank the legal arguments in some order; from strongest to weakest, from most to least recommended.

You can discuss the research base for each item in as much detail as a lawyer reading the file to understand your reasoning might need. In an explanation to a client, however, you should expend most words discussing the most important points and many fewer words on the minor points. Identifying major or minor points in the outline before the first draft saves a lot of typing and deleting.

3.6.5 Fifth, open up options

Common sense used to suggest that a fisherman could best identify where the fish were by looking over the side of the boat. Now fishing fleets locate schools of fish by remote plane or helicopter.

In the name of common sense, we now insist on chaining ourselves to the dictaphone, the word-processor, the library or the note pad. Ironically, like the pilot in the plane or helicopter, sometimes you will only 'see' the facts, the correct formulation of the question, or an elegant satisfactory solution, when you move to a remote location.

We introduce distance in our thinking in socially acceptable ways such as working on more than one piece of work at once, getting up for a cup of coffee, stopping work to go out for a run or a swim, getting up to go out to lunch. Often we will get a flash of insight about the facts, the law, our client's objectives or possible options at the time we have stopped thinking about that particular problem.

If you get 'stuck' but have a tight deadline to meet so that you cannot go for another cup of coffee, you can move your mind back from the problem by giving yourself a thirty second mental holiday. You are now in the helicopter looking for the fish. Open any magazine and leaf through the pictures asking yourself by association if any pictures help your problem. Or you can refer to a dictionary and select a number of words at random. Ask yourself *what do those words suggest about the problem*?

You might feel immediately sceptical about this suggestion. However, life has a way of turning up words and images which are not solutions in themselves but which lead to solutions.

One example from the management of a law firm might encourage you to try. A group of lawyers recently decided that their accounts department staff were not working as hard as was needed. The lawyers were pessimistic about introducing any change to improve the situation. At random they found some production line pictures in a magazine which caused them to ask whether the job could be redesigned to make it more interesting. The words 'hedge' and 'stool pidgeon' appeared in turn from the dictionary. They suggested that accounts department staff might have felt isolated in their dark room in an awful part of the office. The lawyers admitted that often accounts staff were rushed along to do their work urgently when it was the lawyer, not the client, who had manufactured the urgency by starting the job too late. Suddenly some new options for resolving the problem were opened up by making a few changes in work design and office location.

3.6.6 Sixth, some techniques for deciding between options

Decide on the deciding factors For most clients money and time will be very important factors in determining which course of action they will instruct their lawyer to take. The deciding factors may not be included in the client's statement of objectives, and if they are not you should ask. It is important to settle on the client's values, because values are an effective way to pattern information persuasively.

Quantify the likelihood of success Most clients will make a decision on a balance of money, time and likelihood of success. You will need to give careful thought to this balance. Many experienced lawyers express the likelihood of success in rough percentage terms.

List the matters for and against It is helpful to list the pros and cons of all arguments from the perspective of your client, and then from the perspective of the other party. Too often, we assume that a good solution for our client is only available at the cost of a bad solution for the other party. In fact, as the problem-solving approach to negotiation demonstrates, the best solution might be one which is to the benefit of both parties (see 'Negotiation' by Diana Tribe in this series).

Identify facts and assumptions At every point in thinking about the problem, the quality of the information will differ. You will need to identify provable facts and working assumptions. In litigation, it is helpful to identify from the outset what evidence you will need to prove your case. Proof costs money and takes time and these are always factors in the advice.

Rank arguments and objectives A good advice will educate the reader's expectations from the outset about what is realistically achievable. It is helpful to establish your client's strongest arguments and the most realistically achievable objectives. Your instructions should rank the objectives to be achieved.

Know thyself Extrovert personality types often clarify their thoughts and actually make decisions by talking. For extroverts, actually articulating aloud the reasoning process will help the choice between competing options. Everybody can gain a boost of confidence by discussing a problem with someone else who agrees. It is also helpful to be told if the other person disagrees and why. Introvert personality types often require a space of their own and silence to sort out thinking. They dislike brainstorming and prefer not to chat about a topic unless they are well prepared.

3.7   Outlining after thinking

You will know that you have completed your thinking when you can

1   state the question in the clients' or readers' terms

2   if it now seems that the client has asked the wrong or a misleading question, re-state the question correctly

3   list the options and rank them tentatively

4   come to some tentative conclusions about the client's likelihood of success and what you think the client should do

5   establish the structures and patterns in which the various points should be discussed.

The thinking activities described in this Chapter will help you to establish the first four points which will be a sufficient basis for an outline. If your conclusions are tentative, you might need to prepare the thinking or first draft before you can come to firm conclusions about what the reader could or should do. It may be that you need to become more expert in the legal subject area of the problem before you can determine appropriate structures and patterns. For this reason, a later Chapter deals with the question of structure and patterns.

On the assumption that you are now ready to produce an outline or a thinking draft, we shall now turn to a discussion of the basic unit of both composition for the author and of communication with the reader - the paragraph.

3.8   End of chapter references and additional reading

Herrmann, N   *The Creative Brain*
(1989)   Herrmann Books

CHAPTER

4 Managing Paragraphs

Following a paragraph is more like following a dance than a dash. The topic sentence draws a circle and the rest of the paragraph is a pirouette within that circle.

Francis Christensen (1975)

4.1 Fashions in paragraphing

The Bible says that in the beginning there was the word. Then grammar books introduced the sentence. Modern rhetorics now focus on the paragraph. In his essay on the paragraph, Francis Christensen says that the paragraph was first introduced into rhetoric as a unit of discourse in 1866 (Christensen, 1975).

Some grammar books have not yet caught up. They contain rules about what constitutes a sentence but not all set out the rules about paragraphs.

This is unfortunate. Just as a lawyer never had to be taught to write a long sentence, so it can be said that lawyers and law students never produce less than a paragraph on any one point. The paragraph, not the sentence, is the basic unit of thought and of communication in the first draft.

Fashion in writing plays a role in the importance of the paragraph. A modern style favours more frequent paragraphs. Lord Atkin's famous judgment in the case of *Donoghue v Stevenson* [1932] AC 564 is an example of an earlier approach to paragraphing. At page 584, Lord Atkin discusses several cases supporting the view that the manufacturer owed a duty of care. His discussion of these cases is contained in one paragraph over nearly three pages. Then His Lordship discusses the cases which argue against a duty of care. The first case discussed, *Dixon v Bell*, has a paragraph of its own. The other cases are then discussed in one paragraph which lasts more than four pages.

A more modern style would introduce more paragraphs into the same subject-matter. The introduction of more white space in the form of shorter sentences has been found to aid the reader. Likewise, the introduction of more white space in the form of an extra line or paragraph indentation has been found to aid scanning and retrieval. In our own work we paragraph by intuition. In introducing more paragraphs we need to have some guidelines to follow so that change would mean improvement. The guidelines would need to tell us

- whether and when to move to another paragraph
- the order for sentences within a paragraph
- the pattern for paragraphs within a sequence.

This Chapter deals with the first two issues. Chapter Seven deals with paragraph patterns.

4.2   The five laws of the paragraph

Bain set out seven so-called 'laws' for the effective paragraph (Lindemann, 1982). Bain can be summarised as recommending that paragraphs should

1   be divided into a number of valid sentences
2   start with an opening sentence which indicates the scope of the paragraph (often called a topic sentence)
3   contain only one subject-matter
4   order sentences so that

  - ideas are identified as major and minor
  - the relationships between the ideas should be clear and express
  - related ideas are kept together within the paragraph
  - iterations or illustrations of the same idea use common constructions.

As Christensen and Lindemann point out, many of these laws are simply guidelines for the structuring of ideas whether at the level of the sentence, the paragraph, the section, or the whole work. The same guidelines will be met again in other contexts.

None of these 'laws' is immutable. Christensen suggests that it is possible to have a valid paragraph in which the topic sentence appears other than at the beginning. He agrees that it is desirable for the ideas to have some discernible order, but gives examples of valid paragraphs which are illogical. Hence, the delightful description of the paragraph as a dance and the topic sentence as a pirouette. Other research confirms that many authors do not follow any or all of these rules. Lindemann (1982) quotes two studies in which more than 50% of the authors did not use topic sentences at all and one study which said that more than 50% of authors did not order their ideas in accordance with Bain's laws.

But if we are to attempt to improve Lord Atkin's judgment by inserting more paragraphs, and to learn some lessons for our own writing style, a more detailed analysis of the theories of Bain and others might be useful. I have distilled Bain's laws into five simple laws.

4.2.1 First Law

More than one sentence

One of the bases upon which we determine when to move to another paragraph is appearance. Today it would not be common to have a paragraph which covered the whole of a page, unless some tabulation were used. Nor would it be common for a paragraph to consist of one sentence. Nor would it be common for a sentence to lack a verb - the only necessary and sufficient condition for a valid English sentence.

Not common.

But it does happen!

Lord Denning legitimised the use of the sentence without a verb (see, for example, *Lloyds Bank Ltd v Bundy* [1975] QB p 326 at 334). In highly formal works, we would probably still try to ensure that each sentence contains a verb. If an idea can be expressed naturally and clearly without a verb, then such a sentence would be acceptable.

And a one sentence paragraph, used sparingly, can give emphasis to a particularly important idea.

4.2.2 Second Law

A topic sentence

Modern rhetoricians have modified the rigour of Bain's invocation that the topic sentence should appear first. Perhaps this is in recognition of the fact that many admirable authors blissfully ignore this rule.

Business writers, however, often use a topic sentence and place it first. The topic sentence helps the busy business reader maintain concentration on the argument. Placing the topic sentence first also aids scanning and retrieval for particular points. The topic sentence also means that the reader can skip paragraphs which do not contain the answers to specific questions.

Here is an example of a paragraph with the topic sentence placed first

> **Office telephones are meant to be used for office purposes.** Using them privately without consent is essentially no different from taking someone else's money without consent. Even more important, if lines are blocked by private telephone calls they clearly cannot be used for office calls. Most firms do not object to occasional short personal calls being made by members of the firm on the firm's telephone. Likewise, incoming personal calls are generally accepted provided that they are limited in both duration and frequency. It is one thing to take a call to arrange to meet for a drink after work, quite another to gossip for twenty minutes or make a long distance personal call at the firm's expense.

(Shurman, 1989
The Practical Skills of the Solicitor, Oyez Longman)

Topic sentences in legal writing can also be found at the end, in the middle, and split between the beginning and the end of paragraphs, although these positions are rarer.

The following are examples from an editorial on legal writing of paragraphs in which the topic sentences appear other than at the beginning (Wood, 1991). The topic sentences are in bold. Part of a preceding paragraph is set out to retain the sense.

> ... Another side effect of the Roget syndrome is definitionalising. Naturally the colossal dictionary that appears in clause 1 on the credit agreement, finance lease, and other financial document has its uses, even though one has to labour to learn a new private language to understand the agreement. But one has to be pessimistic about the frailty of a language to insist on defining words like 'assets', 'person', 'taxes' ... Part of the motive of definitionalising is to improve protections ...

> This type of shorthand concealing a bombshell is universal. On the one hand the bank is better off. On the other hand the lay borrower may regard this as typical lawyer weasliness. Whatever view one takes about that, the disadvantage is that words no longer mean what they say and this is dangerous for everybody except those who pore over these documents all day. Contracts become a private world, a secret code which only the inner mandarins understand. **They do not take the reader into account.**

> Finally, there is one other constraint. This is that financial agreements have a decorum, a courtesy of style, a ceremony. **Although the world wants simple contracts there is no question that the vernacular is not available. Documents cannot be drafted as people speak.** For example, it is not really possible to draft an insolvency event as, 'The Borrower goes bust'.

Brand and White (1976) cite an extract from the judgment of *Yania v Bigan* 397 Pa 316,155 A.2d 343 as an example of a topic set out in two sentences; one at the beginning and the other at the end of the paragraph. The first states the issue, the second the conclusion.

Appellant initially contends that Yania's descent from the high embankment into the water and the resulting death were caused 'entirely' by the spoken words and blandishments of Bigan delivered at a distance from Yania. The complainant does not allege that Yania slipped or that he was pushed or that Bigan made any physical impact upon Yania. On the contrary, the only inference deducible from the facts alleged in the complain is that Bigan, by employment of cajolery and inveiglement, caused such a mental impact on Yania that the latter was deprived of his volitions and freedom of choice and placed under a compulsion to jump into the water. Had Yania been a child of tender years or mentally deficient then it is conceivable that taunting or enticement could constitute actionable negligence if it resulted in harm. **However, to contend that such conduct directed to an adult in full possession of all his menta! faculties constitutes actionable negligence is not only without precedent but is completely without merit.**

Paragraphs which narrate the chronology of events leading up to an accident often have no topic sentence at all. This is because the narrative sequence makes the topic clear.

Topic sentences assist both the writer and the reader. The topic sentence assists the writer to check that the paragraph deals with the same subject-matter at the same level in the argument (a later rule). The topic sentence assists the reader to concentrate at that point in the argument and to scan a work to find the one or two points of interest to the reader.

Topic sentences at the beginning of the paragraph are easier for both the writer and the reader to find. But we need to bear in mind the need for variety. Variety of expression and of sequencing refresh both the writer and the reader and therefore aid concentration. Variety can be introduced by placing the topic sentence other than at the beginning. It would not be wise, however, to introduce variety by omitting the topic sentence altogether.

4.2.3 Third Law

Unity of subject-matter

One of the most common reasons for editing a paragraph will be that the author will decide, on instinct almost, that some of the subject-matter in a paragraph needs to be moved. It might be better placed in another, existing paragraph. Or it might warrant a new paragraph.

Consider the following paragraph:

> On March 13, 1963 Maryanne Gerardi sustained serious injury as a result of being run over by her neighbour, John Baseltine. The accident occurred just outside Maryanne's family home. She was then just 23 months old. Maryanne had followed Mr Baseltine out of the house after his visit to celebrate the birthday of Maryanne's mother. He had consumed no alcohol. Mr Baseltine was simply unaware of Maryanne's presence. By the time Mr Baseltine drove off, Maryanne had bent over to pick up her doll which had fallen under the car. Mr Baseltine drove over her and did not discover what had happened until he stopped halfway down the street in response to the screams of Maryanne's mother. **Eighteen years later Maryanne still endures the consequences of the accident. Her prognosis suggests that she will still need further plastic surgery to correct scarring on her face; the pelvic injuries sustained mean that if she can conceive, she will only be able to deliver a child by caesarian section.**

The first part of the paragraph deals with the events leading up to the accident. The second deals with the medical consequences and prognosis. They have different places in the narrative and the reader will appreciate that better if they are placed in separate paragraphs.

An idea will not have unity of subject-matter with other ideas in the paragraph where it belongs in a different place in the narrative.

Consider the same paragraph with slight amendment:

> On March 13, 1963 Maryanne Gerardi sustained serious injury
> as a result of being run over by her neighbour, John Baseltine.
> **On August 14, 1973 Mr Baseltine's solicitor on his client's
> behalf admitted liability in a letter**. The accident occurred just
> outside Maryanne's family home. She was then just 23 months
> old. Maryanne had followed Mr Baseltine out of the house after
> his visit to celebrate the birthday of Maryanne's mother. He had
> consumed no alcohol. Mr Baseltine was simply unaware of
> Maryanne's presence. By the time Mr Baseltine drove off,
> Maryanne had bent over to pick up her doll which had fallen
> under the car. Mr Baseltine drove over her and did not discover
> what had happened until he stopped halfway down the street in
> response to the screams of Maryanne's mother.

At one level of generality, it might be said that this paragraph
has unity of subject-matter in that it discusses the facts of the case
as its topic. That Mr Baseltine admitted liability is one of the facts.
Apart from observing that it should have been given in chronological
order, on this view, that fact belongs in this paragraph.

Yet in any legal analysis, the fact of admitting liability is of a
different order from the background events which give rise to the
claim in the first place. This fact belongs more with a discussion of
the legal action which followed rather than with a simple narration
of the accident itself.

Therefore, in addition to unity of narrative, a paragraph should
retain unity of argument. A legal argument is traditionally
formulated in a series of considerations which follow this format:

- a consideration of the background events
- a definition of the client's objectives
- a discussion of the law as applied to the facts and the client's
  objectives
- an assessment of the options open to the client
- a recommendation for action.

Each of these considerations, no matter how shortly expressed,
would normally be found in different paragraphs.

Thus, a paragraph confirming facts should not comment upon how the law applies. Or, a paragraph summarising the legal issues should not re-discuss the first legal issue.

In the previous example, you will remember that the events about the accident were to be separated from the consequences and prognosis. In terms of the relationship of each topic to the argument, the separation of these topics into separate paragraphs is justified. The first topic is relevant to establishing liability, the second and third to an argument about quantum.

Unity of narrative and of argument might sometimes also be extended to unity of communication purpose. You might decide to separate out material into separate paragraphs where the *function* of the material in the explanation differs. Topic material may serve many different functions, for example:

- introduce a new topic
- provide support for a topic (through examples)
- conclude a topic
- act as a transition between topics.

Different functions in the communication may be another reason for moving material out of a paragraph. You might want to divide such a paragraph when the divisions would be helpful for the reader to appreciate the different functions that the material serves in the explanation. The provision of a number of examples in support would also justify the move to another paragraph.

4.2.4 Fourth Law

Clarity of structure

Four of Bain's laws related to clarity of structure. He suggested that

- ideas should be identified as major or minor
- the relationships between the ideas should be clear and express
- related ideas should be kept together within the paragraph
- iterations or illustrations of the same idea should use common constructions.

Christensen has suggested that the only one of these 'laws' which should be treated as a 'rule' is the last; that certain ideas require common constructions. He proposes a tool for analysing structure based on whether the ideas in the paragraph are **co-ordinate** - ideas related by theme or argument but at the same level of generality - or **subordinate** - related ideas at progressively lower levels of generality. In this analysis, sentences are numbered in relation to the level of generality in the argument posed within the paragraph. Such an analysis will reveal how thoughts can be re-ordered or re-written for greater clarity.

The subordinate sequence Here is an example of a subordinate sequence taken from Sir Ernest Gowers' book *The Complete Plain Words*.

Example One

1 American English differs from British English not only in pronunciation but also in some points of spelling, punctuation, syntax and (above all) vocabulary.

   2 It would be absurd for us to assume that an American word, expression, or construction is necessarily better just because it seems novel, or that it is necessarily worse just because we have not encountered it before.

      3 Occasionally what seems an American innovation is in fact an old English usage that has survived across the Atlantic but has been generally abandoned in the land of its origin.

         4 Older usages preserved in American English include *fall* meaning 'autumn', *mad* meaning 'angry', the verb form *gotten* and *loan* as a verb.

(Gowers, 1986)

This is a subordinate structure because it moves from the most general to the most specific. It is not possible to re-order the sentences and to maintain the same sense of coherence. These ideas are ordered as

- a topic sentence about how American English differs from British English

- users of British English (the implied *us*) should not assume that particular differences make American English either worse or better

- some differences are actually examples of archaic British English

- examples of archaic British English use are ...

In business writing, the clearest subordinate structure will give the paragraph a pyramid shape, with the topic sentence expressed first and subordinate ideas ordered from most general to most particular.

The co-ordinate sequence Here is an example of a co-ordinated structure taken from the section on topic sentences.

Example Two

　1　Topic sentences assist both the writer and the reader.

　　　2　The topic sentence assists the writer to check that the paragraph deals with the same subject-matter at the same level in the argument (a later rule).

　　　2　The topic sentence assists the reader to concentrate at that point in the argument and to scan a work to find the one or two points of interest to the reader.

The first sentence is a summary of the paragraph. The second two sentences are at the same level of generality. One gives an example about how a topic sentence can assist the writer. The other gives examples of how the topic sentence can help the reader. The order of the two sentences was determined by the order set by the topic sentence. If the topic sentence had talked about *the reader* and *the writer*, the other sentences could have been reversed.

Christensen is not prescriptive in his analysis of the structure of paragraphs and gives many examples of mixed structures. Mixed structures are very common in law-related works.

Combined structure based on a subordinate sequence

Here is an example of a combined structure based on a subordinate sequence contained in a paragraph already cited.

Example Three

1 Office telephones are meant to be used for office purposes.

   2 Using them privately without consent is essentially no different from taking someone else's money without consent.

   2 Even more important, if lines are blocked by private telephone calls they clearly cannot be used for office calls.

     3 Most firms do not object to occasional short personal calls being made by members of the firm on the firm's telephone.

     3 Likewise, incoming personal calls are generally accepted provided that they are limited in both duration and frequency.

       4 It is one thing to take a call to arrange to meet for a drink after work, quite another to gossip for twenty minutes or make a long distance personal call at the firm's expense.

This is a subordinate structure overall in which the ideas have been ordered as follows:

1 Statement of the rule.

2 Reasons for the existence of the rule.

3 Two exceptions to the rule.

4 Conditions under which the exceptions prevail.

Any other arrangement of the ideas would not have been as clear.

Where there is some subordination of ideas, there should always be a general rationale underlying the order in which ideas are expressed; in this case from an expression of the rule to its exceptions. Other subject-matter might be ordered by cause and effect, deductively (stating the premises and then the conclusion), inductively (stating the conclusion and then giving the supporting evidence), structurally (by reference to an order established in the topic under discussion such as referring to a document in section order or discussing contract law in conventional order), or by applying a particular set of values (from most to least recommended, for example). Christensen rightly observes that these orders are no different for the paragraph than they are for the sub-section, the section or the whole of the work. For that reason, ways of arranging subordinated ideas will be dealt with in Chapter Seven in more detail.

Where there is some co-ordination of ideas at the same level of generality, as in example three above, the careful writer will give some thought to the order of ideas, to the language used, and to the use of expressions highlighting co-ordination. In this paragraph the expressions 'even more important' and 'likewise' have been used in the second sentences in each co-ordinated pair to warn the reader that a further idea at the same level of generality is being added.

So how can this analysis be used to improve sequencing and language? Consider the following paragraph analysed by Lindemann (1982). It uses both subordination and co-ordination.

Example Four

> Dark green, leafy vegetables such as kale and spinach are good sources of Vitamin C and iron. Carrots, squash and sweet potatoes are good sources of carotene, which the body changes to Vitamin A. All vegetables are good for us because they provide important vitamins and minerals that build cells and keep us healthy. Vitamin C, for example, builds strong teeth and helps us resist infection. Vitamin A keeps skin healthy and protects our eyes. Iron, an important part of vegetables, builds red blood cells.

Following the second law, we first find the topic sentence and move it to the front.

> **All vegetables are good for us because they provide important vitamins and minerals that build cells and keep us healthy.** Dark green, leafy vegetables such as kale and spinach are good sources of Vitamin C and iron. Carrots, squash and sweet potatoes are good sources of carotene, which the body changes to Vitamin A. Vitamin C, for example, builds strong teeth and helps us resist infection. Vitamin A keeps skin healthy and protects our eyes. Iron, an important part of vegetables, builds red blood cells.

We then need to analyse the structure of the paragraph to work out which are co-ordinated and which are subordinated ideas.

On one logical analysis, the most general ideas deal with the vitamins that the vegetables contain and the more specific ideas relate to the particular benefits attributable to stated vitamins.

On this analysis, the paragraph is built around the following co-ordinate sequence dealing with the vegetables.

1 **All vegetables are good for us because they provide important vitamins and minerals that build cells and keep us healthy.**

    2 Dark green, leafy vegetables such as kale and spinach are good sources of Vitamin C and iron.

        3 Vitamin C, for example, builds strong teeth and helps us resist infection.

        3 Iron, an important part of vegetables, builds red blood cells.

    2 Carrots, squash and sweet potatoes are good sources of carotene, which the body changes to Vitamin A.

        3 Vitamin A keeps skin healthy and protects our eyes.

On another analysis, the paragraph could be structured on a subordinated sequence, regarding the ideas about vegetables as more general than the information about the benefits of vitamins.

1 **All vegetables are good for us because they provide important vitamins and minerals that build cells and keep us healthy.**

    2 Dark green, leafy vegetables such as kale and spinach are good sources of Vitamin C and iron.

    2 Carrots, squash and sweet potatoes are good sources of carotene, which the body changes to Vitamin A.

        3 Vitamin C, for example, builds strong teeth and helps us resist infection.

        3 Vitamin A keeps skin healthy and protects our eyes.

        3 Iron, an important part of vegetables, builds red blood cells.

On either analysis, the clarity of the paragraph has been improved merely by re-sequencing the sentences.

An analysis of structure will also give you some idea of the language you can use to make the structure and, therefore, the relationships between ideas, clear and express. Out of Bain's (see para 4.2 above) rules on paragraphing structure, I have derived the fifth law of the paragraph.

4.2.5 Fifth Law

Signpost content and relationship

Analysis will help you re-order the ideas in a paragraph so that the subordinate relationships are ordered from the general to the particular and so that the co-ordinate relationships are grouped together appropriately.

The relationships can be revealed even more clearly by the use of certain language which you might think of as a *signpost*. Sometimes the signpost will be in the topic sentence; sometimes the signpost will be contained in the language or structure of other sentences.

Signposts for subordinated ideas There are at least three common ways in which ideas are expressed in subordination: to show connection in logical argument; to specify a rule and exceptions; and to give examples.

Words showing connections in logical argument between ideas are words such as *because* or *therefore*.

The specification of a *rule and exception* is another example of a subordinate relationship. It is often helpful to state expressly that you are setting out a rule and then to say that you are setting out the exceptions or qualifications.

The giving of examples and the articulation of relationships introduced by words such as *which, that, who* will also highlight subordinate relationships. In the paragraph on vegetables, the sentence about Vitamin C is reinforced as an example by the use of the words 'for example'. Where more than one example is given, it can often be helpful to signpost the number, as well as the fact of giving examples.

Signposts for co-ordinated ideas In a co-ordinate sequence, it is important that the ideas repeat the structure and language set by the topic sentence. First, in the paragraph about the use of topic sentences (see example two above), the structure of the paragraph is determined by the reference to writer and then to the reader. The language of *writer* and *reader* used in the topic sentence is repeated in the next two sentences. Elegant variation adopting *author* and *audience* would have been possible but would have muddied the recognition by the reader that the ideas are co-ordinated. Both sentences are introduced with the expression '*the topic sentence assists*' so that the ideas are marked as a co-ordinate sequence.

In the paragraph on vegetables (example four above), the sentences beginning with vegetables are structured in the same way as are the sentences dealing with vitamins. It would have been possible to convey the same sense but to have varied the order of the language. Similarity of structure in each sentence helps us to identify that the level of generality of ideas in the explanation is similar.

Where the topic sentence does not specify the co-ordination, the sentences expressing co-ordinate ideas should have some features of structure and language in common. In the paragraph on office phone calls (example three above), the writer emphasises co-ordinate relationships by the expressions 'even more important' and 'likewise'.

Lawyers examine the same point from the perspective of all parties and therefore legal argument requires many co-ordinated sequences. Co-ordinated sequences are often represented by expressions such as *and, or, but, however, either, or, either, neither, on the one hand, on the other hand*.

In the rush to shorten sentences, avoid the temptation to take out these signposts. Signposts help knit the narrative into the argument and to structure both the narrative and the argument into a clear communication.

4.3 From the general to the particular

Having considered the five laws of the paragraph, we shall now move to considerations about how to manage the next unit of expression: the sentence.

4.4 End of chapter references and additional reading

Bain, A A (1866)	*English Composition and Rhetoric* Oxford University Press
Brand, N and White, J (1976)	*Legal Writing: The Strategy of Persuasion* St Martin's Press Inc
Christensen, F (1975)	*A Generative Rhetoric of the Paragraph, Contemporary Rhetoric, Conceptual Background with Readings* W Ross Winterowd ed Harcourt Brace Javanovich
Gowers, E (1986)	*The Complete Plain Words* revised by Greenbaum S and Whitcut J 3rd edition HMSO
Lindemann (1982)	*A Rhetoric for Writing Teachers* 2nd edition Oxford University Press
Shurman, L (1989)	*The Practical Skills of the Solicitor* Oyez Longman
Wood, P R (1991)	*The Lawyer and the Poet* Journal of International Banking and Finance Law Butterworths

CHAPTER

5 Managing Sentences

T'was brillig, and the slithy toves
Did gyre and gimble in the wabe;
All mimsy were the borogroves
And the mome raths outgrabe.

Jabberwocky
Lewis Carroll
Through the Looking Glass

5.1 The gawky sentence

Why do we 'understand' the poem *Jabberwocky*? Probably for several reasons. First, the adjectives and nouns might be nonsense, but they do have an English ring to them - 'slithy toves' and 'brillig'. Second, the verbs and the words that join the nouns to the verbs are definitely not nonsense. Third, and most importantly, the words appear in an order which is recognisably English.

The Bible tells us that in the beginning there was the word. It was probably a subject. We do not know when the subject was joined by a verb. Whenever it was, the sentence appeared. With the joining of words came the concept of grammar and 'correct' syntax. However else you could describe *Jabberwocky*, certainly its syntax is not gawky.

Strictly speaking, a verb alone can constitute a sentence in English. Thus 'Go!' is a proper English sentence. This is a minimalist sentence. As far as written usage is concerned, you are more likely to find a minimalist sentence without a verb, than consisting of a verb alone. Much more likely.

History does not tell us whether the lawyer is solely responsible for the long sentence. Certainly, lawyers are infamous for writing long sentences. Considerable thought and effort, however, has been expended in teaching lawyers how to write short sentences. The tendency of lawyers, along with bureaucrats and politicians, to add things to a sentence rather than to put a full stop, accounts for some of the errors common to legal writing. In short, when lawyers expand their sentences beyond stating subject and verb things often go wrong.

This Chapter concentrates on how to arrange your work so that most sentences are short; and how to manage other, longer sentences. Before moving to the main theme, here is a short list of common errors in sentence construction which you might like to add to your list of things to notice when you revise a draft. They can appear whether the sentence is long or short, but are more likely to demand attention in a long sentence.

The suggestions later in the Chapter about long and short sentences deal with style. The suggestions below deal with grammatical or legal errors as well as style.

5.2   Faults common to sentences long and short

These are dealt with under three headings: problems with verbs; problems with modifying or adding to sentences; and problems with the use of the double negative (write in the positive!).

5.2.1 Problems with verbs: missing, passive, disagreeable and divided

- **Missing: a main verb is required to express the main idea in a sentence**

Sometimes legal sentences start off being so long that the author divides the ideas into more than one sentence. One idea ends up as an incomplete sentence.

> Pursuant to a section 14(1) of the *Finance Act* requiring a person to lodge a return annually.

The author might have wished just to state what that section of the Act requires, in which case the sentence should read:

> Section 14(1) of the *Finance Act* requires a person to lodge a return annually.

If the author wished to go on and make another major point about the section, then the full stop needed to be changed into a comma and the thought should have continued.

> Pursuant to a section 14(1) of the *Finance Act* requiring the lodgement of an annual return, penalties of up to $100,000 or three years' imprisonment can be imposed.

The quotation of sections and cases is the most frequent instance in which authors produce a fragmentary sentence. The author is preoccupied in paraphrasing the content of the section and fails to appreciate that the sentence requires a main verb or a further statement. These errors escape proof-reading with surprising frequency.

- **Passive**

The passive describes one of the two voices of verbs. The most common voice is the *active*: for example, *Jonathan signed the contract*. The passive voice reverses the normal order. The verb is combined with the verb *to be*: for example, *the contract was signed by Jonathan*.

There are two problems with the passive voice. First, the subject who is to perform the action can be left out entirely and the sentence is still perfectly correct in grammar: for example, *the contract was to be signed by Monday*. A secondary stylistic consideration is that the constant use of the passive voice makes the prose impersonal, cold and gives the reader the impression that the author is ducking responsibility.

> It has been decided that the highest amount you are likely to be offered in compensation for the loss of your right arm is considerably less than that which was advised originally.

Who decided and why? Doesn't the lawyer realise that this amount of compensation will be the only financial security a client who can no longer work will have?

- **Disagreeable: a verb should agree with its subject in number**

  While discussion between aggrieved parties are preferable to
  instant recourse to the courts, there is something unpalatable
  about the recent spate of court settlements.

This should read *discussion ... is preferable*. The verb has
taken on the colour of the noun immediately preceding with the
result that a plural verb sounds almost correct.

  None of the arguments are acceptable.

A similar mistake. *None* takes a singular verb. This should read:

  None of the arguments is acceptable.

You should also check verbs which follow *who* or *that*
expressions.

  Jonathan is among the few able lawyers who has succeeded
  in politics.

This should read *who have* to agree with *lawyers*.

  This is one of the most illogical arguments that has ever
  been made.

This should read *that have* to agree with *arguments*.

Finally, you should always check that there is agreement
between introducing words and enumerated instances. Writers
often tend to get the first three or so correct, but then
disagreement appears.

  The specific allegations of fraud against the defendant include:

  1 falsely stating that the sworn market value of the property
     was $250,000

  2 failing to state that the dishwasher and antique light fittings
     were not the property of the defendant

  3 to represent that the house was authentic Federation period.

This should read:

  3 representing that the house was ...

There are other occasions in which subjects and verbs fail
to agree but these are the most common in my experience
(for others, see Rooke, 1983).

- **Divided: parts of the verb should be kept together**

The writ issued by Mr Walter Leechman on behalf of Mrs May Donoghue described the factory where the ginger beer was bottled as a place where *'snails and the slimy trails of snails were frequently found'* (The Paisley Papers (1991)).

Undoubtedly ahead of his time, Mr Leechman's drafting was perfectly in synchrony with the style of his peers: lawyers split parts of the verb with surprising frequency and thereby rob the refining adverb of its impact. The expression *'snails and slimy trails of snails were found frequently'* would have given the claim the emphasis that the House of Lords subsequently supplied.

It is good practice to keep parts of the verb together. This practice should include grouping the prepositions that accompany the verb with the parts of the verb. But we don't always do this. Sorry, we don't do this always. Certainly it is more necessary sometimes than others.

> More specifically, lawyers have been accused of failing to sensibly group verbs together and of failing to meticulously keep infinitives together. They have often answered this accusation by resolutely stating that the content requires the peculiar writing style. They have, with the best possible intention, resisted this advice on Plain English for a long time.

This paragraph can be improved in a number of ways. A major improvement, though, would be to place all the parts of verbs together. The parts of the verb are highlighted.

> More specifically, lawyers have been accused of *failing to group* verbs together sensibly and *of failing to keep* infinitives together meticulously. They *have answered* this accusation often *by stating* resolutely that the content requires the peculiar writing style. They *have resisted* this advice on Plain English, with the best possible intentions, for a long time.

This rule is an expansion on the rule *never to split an infinitive*. The better rule is that the meaning of verbs is understood more readily when all parts of the verb and accompanying prepositions stay together. The adverb which qualifies the verb also enjoys more emphasis when it is placed before or after the verb expression.

Qualifying phrases or clauses will achieve more prominence when they are not placed in the middle of a verb expression.

If you have difficulty moving the adverbs around, it might be that there are too many. The example given above would be improved by deleting some of the adverbs. Deletion of adjectives and adverbs is one of the strategies for shortening sentences and for simplifying ideas recommended in Chapter Six.

5.2.2 Modifying or adding to sentences

The sentence grows as we add additional information or qualify that which is already there.

• **The run on sentence without comma or full stop**

A run on sentence is technically one which requires a full stop between two ideas. The term is used here to include sentences which omit commas incorrectly. Commas are dealt with first.

The legal maxim that commas cause ambiguity is unfortunate. We routinely produce sentences such as this.

> We suggest therefore that the payment which could properly be characterised as an *ex gratia* payment should attract minimal tax liability unless the Commissioner considers the underlying claim an enforceable contract.

Otherwise this sentence might be punctuated as follows:

> We suggest, therefore, that the payment, which could properly be characterised as an *ex gratia* payment, should attract minimal tax liability, unless the Commissioner considers the underlying claim an enforceable contract.

If commas are left out, the sentences are harder to scan and the effort of scanning slows the reader.

Perhaps as an extension of its disapproval of the comma, legal writing also often features the omission of the full stop.

> Although a guarantor may give a guarantee to ensure that a customer is granted a particular loan the discharge of the loan does not release the guarantor the personal obligations and collateral given under the guarantee will still apply.

This should read:

> Although a guarantor may give a guarantee to ensure that a customer is granted a particular loan, the discharge of the loan does not release the guarantor. The personal obligations and collateral given under the guarantee will still apply.

- **Identifying personal pronouns**

> From the transcript of evidence it is clear that the bank manager assisted the guarantor to execute the guarantee validly and then he left the room.

Who left the room? The guarantor or the bank manager?

The use of relative pronouns can be ambiguous. It can be avoided if more short sentences are used which usually force the writer to specify the subject.

- **Misplaced modifiers**

If additional information is added in the wrong place, confusion or ambiguity can result.

In books of grammar or usage, the most frequent examples given are those illustrating the possible misuse of modifying words like *just* or *only*. In the example below, the modifying word 'only' appears in four different positions in the sentence, resulting in four different meanings.

> Only one witness told my Counsel what he had seen. (*The other witnesses told what they had heard.*)

> One witness told only my Counsel what he had seen. (*Other witnesses involved in my case told people other than Counsel.*)

> One witness told my Counsel what only he had seen. (*He saw something that other witnesses had not.*)

> One witness told my Counsel what he had only seen. (*He did not relate information about what he heard or what he had been told about.*)

In my experience, the misplaced phrase or clause is more common.

Here is an example of a misplaced clause:

> Sections 72(3) and 72(4) provide for the execution as deeds of certain classes of contracts which were recently amended.

The *sections*, presumably, were recently amended, not *the contracts to be executed as deeds*.

An example of a misplaced phrase:

> You could make a tax deductible gift to a school, hospital or community project within the definition of a charitable institution.

Do the *school*, *hospital* and *community project* have to fall within the definition of *charitable institution*, or does this phrase modify *community project* only?

If the modification is to *community project* only, the sentence could be rephrased to place *school* and *hospital* last. If the phrase modifies all three then the more general definition should come first followed by the examples.

> You could make a tax deductible gift to a charitable institution as defined such as a hospital, school or community project.

5.2.3 Write in the positive

Lawyers frequently follow the exhortation to write in the positive only by creating a positive idea out of a double negative. In formal speeches this is often used by way of modest understatement and can be quite appropriate.

> And now it falls upon us to congratulate Sir Norman Dithers for his not inconsiderable efforts in assisting the Foundation by raising funds.

In business communications, however, the double negative should be replaced by the positive.

> The plaintiff was not unaware that she took some risk in relying on the defendant's advice, given that she knew his inexperience in this type of transaction.

Without change of meaning this reads more clearly as:

> The plaintiff was aware that she took some risk relying on the defendant's advice, given that she knew his inexperience in this type of transaction.

Often an affirmative substitute can be found for commonly used negative expressions. Williams (1985) gives a list from which the following examples are in common legal usage:

not many	few
not the same	different
not different	alike/similar
did not	failed to
does not have	lacks
did not stay	left
did not remember	forgot
did not consider	ignored
had nothing to do with	avoided
did not allow	prevented
did not accept	rejected

5.3   In praise of the short sentence

One of the cornerstones of all brands of Plain English is the short sentence. For legal writing *short* means a sentence of 20 words or less. Using short sentences will force the writer to clarify ideas and relationships between ideas. This Chapter will give you some techniques for shortening sentences.

Writers often expect the consistent use of short sentences to reduce the number of words used to express their ideas. In fact, the use of a majority of short sentences will often increase overall word length. For example, by creating two (longer) sentences out of the above paragraph we can reduce its overall length from 50 words (the short sentence version) to 44.

> One of the cornerstones of all brands of Plain English is the short sentence; using 20 words or less. This Chapter will give you some techniques for shortening sentences so that you will force yourself to clarify your ideas and the relationships between them (44 words).

So, shorter sentences do not necessarily mean fewer words.

If the audience is well-educated or belongs to the same profession, why use short sentences? We live, after all, in an environmentally sensitive age where consumption of paper should be a concern. The answer is simple. Sentence beginnings and endings are points of emphasis. The more beginnings and endings in a text, the greater number of points of emphasis. Ideas buried in the middle of long sentences can be missed by the reader. The reader will comprehend a greater number of your ideas if you increase the ratio of sentences to ideas. *Brevity* is a virtue desirable in legal writing; *clarity* is a still higher virtue.

Clarity will be of supreme importance in introductions, transitions between sections and in conclusions. At these times the short sentence is indispensable.

5.4   Techniques for shortening sentences

5.4.1 One idea per sentence

- **Delete the co-ordinate *and***

One idea per sentence is in fact a rule of grammar. Lawyers like to add to ideas (a co-ordinate sequence) often in the same sentence. You can delete the *and* between two ideas of equal importance where both warrant emphasis and form two sentences.

> Not: Practice of the law today is difficult and successful
>   practice is extremely challenging.

> But: Practice of the law today is difficult. Successful practice
>   is challenging.

- **Begin a new sentence with *but***

One of the few rules of grammar many lawyers believe they remember includes the injunction not to begin a sentence with *and* or *but*. But this is not a rule of grammar; it is even doubtful as a rule of style.

Sir Ernest Gowers begins sentences with 'but' frequently. For example,

> Two points are worth making.
>
> One is to give a warning against over-indulgence in the trick of encasing words or phrases in inverted commas to indicate that they are being used in slang or technical or facetious or some other unusual sense. This is a useful device; instances may be found in this book. But it is a dangerous habit

> Sir Ernest Gowers
> *The Complete Plain Words* (1991)

- **Remember 'The cat sat on the mat'**

You can also follow the rule one idea, one sentence by following the syntax of the simple sentence: *subject* plus *verb* plus *object*. As soon as many sentences commence with a qualification, you risk drowning the ideas in the words.

This formula is particularly important in introductions, transitions between points and in conclusions where you want the reader to concentrate the most. Consider the following introductory sentence:

> Under section 14 (1) of the *Finance Act 1985*, in any case where, for a prescribed accounting period, a return is made which understates a person's liability to tax or overstates his entitlement to a payment, the person concerned shall be liable, subject to sections (6) & (7), to a penalty equal to 30% of tax which would have been lost had the inaccuracy not been discovered.

This sentence contains many ideas.

1 Section 14 of the Finance Act 1985 creates a penalty both for understating liabilities and for overstating entitlement to payment in a return in relation to any given accounting period.

2 The penalty is equal to 30% of tax which would have been lost had the inaccuracy not been discovered.

3 That penalty increases if there are inaccuracies in returns over two accounting periods or more. (This is an additional piece of information, inserted here to account for the use of the expression *for a prescribed accounting period* in the original.)

4 The person liable to pay the penalty is *the person concerned* which is defined in the Act and normally will be the tax payer.

5 *The person concerned* might be able to use the defences contained in sub-sections (6) and (7).

Statements of law often require two subjects, for two separate sentences. The first subject will be the section or case and its rule. The second subject will be the person it affects and a statement of what they must do or how they are affected. Stating the law first and then stating how it affects people is a natural order.

The rewritten sentence about the Finance Act is another example of how a change to short sentences might increase the number of words overall. I hope you agree, though, that the increase in clarity makes the cost justifiable.

5.4.2 Reduce the number of prepositions and conjunctions

In Northern Australia the cane toad has reached plague proportions. I heard a report on the radio recently about efforts of scientists to find a biological means of eradicating this pest.

The scientist said:

> We are looking for a virus which will do for the cane toad what myxoma did for the rabbit in the '50s.

In describing the relationship between myxoma and the rabbit, the scientist unintentionally changed the meaning by using the wrong preposition. I am sure that myxoma does nothing *for* rabbits at all. But it does plenty *to* them; it kills them, painfully and quickly.

Legal reasoning similarly requires us to state relationships between the law and people, the law and events. Relationship words are prepositions (*to, of, from, about*) and conjunctions (*and, unless, but*).

The most difficult aspect of learning English for non-native speakers is mastering prepositions. First language English speakers still have trouble. Does one say different *to* or different *from* ? Aim *for* or aim *at* ? Suffer *with* or suffer *from*? (The latter are all the correct versions.)

Reading legal English is a real challenge for non-native speakers because lawyers seem to prefer expressions which require lots of prepositions. In the following sentence the prepositions are highlighted.

> *In* these circumstances, it is appropriate *for* the legal profession *to* assert its right *to* determine the standards *of* prospective entrants *to* the profession *by* declining *to* recognise the adequacy *of* training offered *by* institutions which are inadequately resourced.

There are a total of ten prepositions in this sentence. If you identify a high number of prepositions in a sentence, this might mean that sentence should be re-written to express the ideas more crisply or more forcefully. Preposition-rich expressions are often used with the passive voice (as, for example, in this sentence; see para 5.2.1 above) so that the author is able to express a personal opinion but place it in the third person (presumably because it will appear more objective). If we are willing to express thoughts a little more directly we can avoid this long concatenation of expressions requiring prepositions. In the revision, we will also honour some of other basic rules such as one idea per sentence. A crisp revision of this sentence suggests the omission of some words, too.

> In these circumstances the legal profession should refuse to accept the qualifications of institutions which are inadequately resourced. It is appropriate, after all, for the legal profession to determine the standard of its prospective entrants for itself.

The number of prepositions in these *two* sentences has now shrunk from ten to seven.

5.4.3 Transform statements into questions

Have you ever watched an audience's reaction to a speaker's question? The eyes unglaze, the shoulders square, legs uncross and attention is re-focused on the speaker. This technique works for the written word, too.

One of the tenets of Plain English drafting is to use headings in the form of questions. Readers come to a text with questions, seeking answers. If the writer poses the questions that the reader has in mind, then the reader will be able to find the answers more quickly.

A text expounding the law is not necessarily about questions. One can write a lengthy treatise on the law without posing one question. Legal advice, though, is about posing the right questions and suggesting a range of probable answers. As a discipline for thinking before writing, if you pose both the client's questions and the legal issues in question form, you will find that the answers will appear in shorter sentences and in a more logical sequence. For example,

> The facts as given raise questions about whether unjust enrichment might apply, what defences might be open to the purchaser and the remedies which might be available to you.

This sentence certainly works. However, the following version, using rhetorical questions, works better.

> The facts as given raise the following questions:
> 1   Does unjust enrichment apply here?
> 2   What defences might be available to the purchaser?
> 3   What remedies are available to you?

5.5   Techniques for managing the long sentence

We need not abandon the use of long sentences entirely in our desire to increase the frequency of short sentences.

In legal exposition, application and argument, it is not desirable to use short sentences alone.

The succinctness of the paragraph that includes a few well-ordered long sentences is welcome. So is the variety of expression.

Nor will short sentences always be possible. A long sentence often illustrates the relationship between ideas more clearly than a series of short sentences dealing with the same ideas.

This Chapter, therefore, also offers some techniques for the proper control of long sentences.

5.5.1 Put subordinate information in parenthesis

In The Marre Committee Report on The Future of the Legal Profession (1988) an appendix contains a Note of Dissent on rights of audience in the Crown Courts.

> 9.2 If, contrary to our recommendation, the majority's view that rights of audience should be extended to solicitors in the Crown Courts is adopted, we accept that it is essential that those rights should not be exercised by any solicitor who had not satisfied an appropriate body that he was sufficiently skilled for the purpose.

In this sentence there are three ideas.

1   The acknowledgement of the majority view that rights of audience should be extended to solicitors in the Crown Courts.

2   The acceptance that the majority view might be adopted.

3   The opinion that before exercising the right of audience a solicitor should satisfy an appropriate body that he is sufficiently skilled.

This sentence would be rendered clearer by simply re-ordering, re-punctuating, and adding parenthesis.

> If the majority's view that rights of audience should be extended to solicitors in the Crown Courts is adopted (contrary to our recommendation), *we accept that it is essential that* those rights should not be exercised by any solicitor who had not satisfied an appropriate body that he was sufficiently skilled *for the purpose.*

This sentence could be shortened by the deletion of the italicised words which arguably add nothing, but the re-ordering of the phrases alone is an improvement.

5.5.2 Use parallel expressions

The grouping of similar ideas using parallel word order and mirroring parts of speech is a graceful and efficient way to make a point. You have a range of stylistic options here.

- **Group by repeating the whole infinitive form**

This need not be complex. The simple repetition of the whole infinitive form of the verb is commonly overlooked, yet is an important form of parallelism.

> Not: We immediately sought to uncover the extent of the wrongdoing and identify the wrongdoers.

> But: We immediately sought *to* identify the extent of the wrongdoing and *to* identify the wrongdoers.

- **Group by using the same parts of speech in a list**

This can involve a conscious selection of the same part of speech, expressed as a simple list.

In his judgment on the question of the domicile of Errol Flynn at the date of his death, Sir Robert Megarry did not say:

> When he was seventeen he was expelled from school in Sydney, and during the next 33 years, he lived a lusty and full life which was also colourful, if restless.

But said:

> When he was seventeen he was expelled from school in Sydney, and in the next 33 years he lived a life which was full, lusty, restless and colourful.

(In *Re Flynn* [1968] 1 WLR 103 at 105)

Note that the adjectives were ordered from shortest to longest.

- **Group by repeating the whole phrase or clause, changing only the last word or two**

Sometimes the repetition of the same form can add an opportunity for enjoyable, if unexpected, humour.

In *Re Flynn*, Sir Robert Megarry went on to say:

> In his career, in his three marriages, in his friendships, in his quarrels, and in bed with the many women he took there, he lived with zest and irregularity.

- **Group by repeating the structure of the phrase or clause**

Sir Ernest Gowers (*The Complete Plain Words*, 1991) did not say:

> The responsibility of the parliament is to make laws which are then for the executive to administer and afterwards such laws must be interpreted by the judges.

But said:

> It is for the parliament to make laws, for the executive to administer them, and for the judiciary to interpret them.

Parallel forms can be built up in many ways. In the Gower example, the formula is *noun* plus *infinitive form of the verb* plus *object*, and is repeated. Certain expressions will force you to adopt these constructions. Parallel expressions include:

Either ... or

Neither ... nor

Not only ... but

On the one hand ... on the other hand

Both ... and.

These are used most gracefully when the syntax is repeated.

> Not: The lawyer told his secretary to either staple the document or to bind it.

> But: The lawyer told his secretary either to staple the document or to bind it.

Another reason for preferring the second version is that it keeps all parts of the verb together.

> Not: All trainee solicitors are entitled to both four weeks' holiday and five days' study leave.

> But: All trainee solicitors are entitled both to four weeks' holiday and to five days' study leave.

The repetition of syntax here also avoids ambiguity.

- **Group by using 'that' constructions**

In a rare long sentence in a judgment full of short sentences, Lord Denning iterates subordinate clauses beginning with *that* as another form of parallel construction.

> He said that during the first period, Mr Vandervell had an equitable interest in the property, namely, a resulting trust; that he never disposed of this equitable interest (because he never knew that he had it): and that in any case it was the disposition of an equitable interest which, under section 53 of the Law of Property Act 1925, had to be in writing, signed by him or his agent, lawfully authorised by him in writing ...

(In *Re Vandervell's Trusts* (No 2) [1974] Ch 269 at 320)

- **Group by using the colon or semi-colon with other parallel forms**

In his judgment on the question of the domicile of Errol Flynn, Sir Robert Megarry uses the semi-colon as a fulcrum around which to balance his consideration of both sides of the argument. The semi-colon is accompanied by examples where the whole infinitive form of the verb is repeated and of other forms of parallel syntax. It is an excellent example of sustained parallelism.

> During the last year and a half of his life, Errol (as I shall call him) wrote an autobiography which in England was published shortly after his death under the title 'My Wicked Wicked Ways.' ... Ungoed-Thomas J directed that this book was to be admitted as evidence subject to Mr Conrad verifying the statements in it made by Errol; and this Mr Conrad duly did. I have been referred to a number of specific passages and I have also looked through the book as a whole. Errol would, I think, have been the last person to claim that it was a serious study. It is plainly a book

> intended to entertain and to sell; and I do not doubt that it has done both. I am not covertly suggesting that what is said in the book is untrue; but truth is many-sided, and a wrong impression is perhaps more often conveyed by what is omitted than by what is said. Nor is it unknown that, in the telling, a story intended to entertain should grow and be refined. The semblance between a tombstone and an autobiography may not be very close; but just as in lapidary inscriptions a man is not upon oath, so may autobiographies, even though verified on the oath of a collaborator, fail accurately to convey the truth, the whole truth, and nothing but the truth as the author knows it.

(In *Re Flynn* [1968] 1 WLR 103 at 105, 106)

The need to set out both sides of the argument is a common one in legal writing. Comparisons and contrasts balance well and clearly around colons and semi-colons.

5.5.3 Set out multiple ideas visually

Once you are or become accustomed to using long sentences and parallel constructions, you will find that the meaning will be conveyed with even greater ease if the long sentence is tabulated in some way. Two forms of tabulation used much in drafting are now more frequent in writing: bullet points and numbering.

- **Bullet points**

These can be used where focus is on the ideas and the sequence is less important.

> There are some key steps to be taken in investigating the purchase of a property. Before signing the contract, the potential purchaser should have
>
> - personally inspected the property more than once
> - measured the boundaries of the property as fenced
> - checked that the boundaries as fenced conform to the boundaries given on the title
> - discussed finance with the bank manager
> - decided that the likely legal costs, fees, duties and the level of monthly repayments for the next couple of years are within budget.

- **Numbers**

These can be used where not only the ideas and but also the sequence are both important.

Please take the following steps in signing the will:

1   Have the two independent adult witnesses in the room with you until this whole procedure is complete.

2   Read the will carefully.

3   Ensure that it complies with your intention.

4   Sign the will with your usual signature where indicated in the presence of both witnesses.

5   Have each witness sign where indicated in the presence of the other witness and you.

6   As a courtesy for later people referring to the will, have the witnesses print their full names, addresses and occupations beneath their names where indicated.

Other kinds of visual representation which are useful in setting out advice include

- flow charts to set out procedures

- decision charts setting out the decision-making process in a hierarchical series of questions each capable only of a yes/no answer

- classification tables when dealing with interlocking definitions or classes with varying attributes

- time lines to set out the significant steps in large processes.

5.6   End of chapter references and additional reading

Gowers, E
(1991)
The Complete Plain Words
Revised by Greenbaum, S and Whitcut, J
3rd edition
HMSO

The Marre Committee
(1988)
A Time for Change
Report of the Committee on the Future
of the Legal Profession
The General Council of the Bar
The Law Society of England and Wales

The Paisley Papers
(1991)
*Donoghue v Stevenson and the
Modern Law of Negligence*
Proceedings of the Continuing
Education Society of British Columbia
Blackstone Press

Rooke, CT
(1983)
*Advanced Errors: A Grammar
Instruction Booklet*
Minter Ellison Morris Fletcher
with the permission of the
Continuing Legal Education Society of
British Columbia

Williams, J M
(1985)
Style Ten Lessons in Clarity and Grace
2nd edition
Scott, Foresman and Company

CHAPTER

6 Choosing Words

It don't mean a thing if it ain't got that swing

Popular song

6.1 The language of oligarchy

You will know when you have passed the threshold of initiation into the practice of the legal profession. Legal writing has a kind of rhythm which is different from other prose. Long sentences sprinkled liberally with long words will give your prose that law-swing.

The appeal to feeling as well as to thought used to be what lawyers had in common with priests. Reading legal language was like taking part in a kind of mystery, only part of which was capable of being rendered into logical meaning.

Two examples of the old forms of legal documents follow, which eloquently illustrate this point. Be prepared, however, for the language of these examples to sound familiar. They are followed by two further examples which are taken from letters, written over 150 years ago. Strictly speaking, legal drafting falls outside the scope of this book (see 'Drafting' by Elmer Doonan in this series) but these examples of drafting provide excellent examples of the language of oligarchy.

The Writ of Attachment for the Supreme Court of Victoria, Australia, used until 1990, demonstrates the characteristic use of antique words in antique ways.

> Elizabeth the Second, by the Grace of God Queen of Australia and all Her other Realms and Territories, Head of the Commonwealth,
>
> To the Sheriff, Greeting:
>
> We command you to attach [the Defendant], so as to have him before us in our Supreme Court, there to answer us, as well

> touching a contempt which he it is alleged hath committed
> against us, as also such other matters as shall be then and
> there laid to his charge, and further to perform and abide such
> order as our said Court shall make in this behalf; and hereof,
> fail not, and bring this writ with you.

This is an odd mixture of formality and farce. You can just
picture the Sheriff sitting on his horse and riding off into the
sunset, clutching the writ with him, mindful of the invocation to
bring the writ (which seems added as an afterthought, in
disarmingly modern language).

Much of the formal language is excusable given that it is
expressed to be in the voice of the Sovereign.

The draftsperson has mangled the word order in such a way
that the stately progress of the ideas is disturbed. The expression
it is alleged is plunged right into the middle of *he hath committed*
in the worst legal style, without even the pair of commas to signal
an interpolation. Worse, the expression *perform and abide* reads
as a redundant pair using the expression *abide by*, in the sense of
'abide by the Court order', but with the unfortunate omission of the
necessary preposition. Re-ordered as *abide and perform*, it is
then clear that neither word is redundant; the Sheriff is
commanded to stay at Court and to perform further orders that the
Court might require.

Even if the word order is not in disarray, as in this example,
when we start to use such language for workaday things, both
writer and reader can easily become confused.

The first sentence of a Power of Attorney used to be:

KNOW YE ALL MEN

> To whom these presents shall come. I, Jarryd Luke Jones of
> Flat 3 Borstall Street, Glasgow do hereby constitute and
> appoint etc.

The conferring of a power of attorney by a duke might have
meant at one time the right to make decisions affecting the lives
of hundreds of people and thousands of pounds. For most of us,

however, this grand announcement usually amounts to a more mundane reality, for example deputising someone else to pay our household bills in our absence. In a democratic society, the purpose of the law is not to entrench the power and perquisites of a grand few, thus protecting their property from the depredations of the many. It is to enable the average law-abiding citizen to go about life without undue attack by government or felon. Grand, ceremonious language is out of place.

Undemocratic relationships between author and recipient are clear in the correspondence of the 19th century. Take, for example, the following two short letters, in which William Lonsdale and Foster Fyans formally set out the plight of convicts shipped to Australia in the first half of the 19th century (from the Public Record Office, Victoria Foundation Series 1981 Vol 1).

> William Lonsdale to the Colonial Secretary
> 6 November 1838
>
> In reply to your letter of the 17th ult. which I had the honour to receive yesterday, I beg to state for the information of His Excellency the Governor that there is scarcely any land under cultivation in this district. A few settlers have put in a small quantity of grain, but not sufficient to calculate upon as a general supply, and in fact in no instance sufficient for the individual's own station consumption.
>
> There is no grain remaining unconsumed as we have not yet obtained our supply of flour from either Sydney or Van Dieman's Land.
>
> Foster Fyans to the Colonial Secretary
> 19 February 1838
>
> For His Excellency's information, I beg to state that the winter season in this place is extremely cold and damp, and trust that the warm clothing for the convicts of this establishment may be furnished as soon as possible, and beg leave to recommend that the shoes should be of a better and more lasting description than what is generally furnished, as we have no means of repairing them.

Undoubtedly expressions such as *I beg leave to recommend* had reached the level of cliche even in those times so the authors may not have intended to be begging at all. Nor would their recipients have seen them as doing so. The persistence of such expressions, even as cliche, reminds us of the stark inequalities which historically often existed between writer and reader. Hopefully, the relationship today is more often an equal one. Where the relationship has changed so should the form and language.

6.2   The language of democracy

Great writers in this century recognised that the onset of democracy required a change of register and diction before lawyers. Today a writer who admires Shakespeare is more likely to write like Samuel Beckett:

> They clothed me and gave me money. I knew what the money was for, it was to get me started. When I was gone I would have to get more, if I wanted to go on. The same for the shoes, when they were worn out I would have to get them mended, or get myself another pair, or go on barefoot, if I wanted to go on. The same for the coat and trousers, needless to say, with this difference that I could go on in my short sleeves if I wanted. The clothes - shoes, socks, trousers, shorts, coat, hat - were not new, but the deceased must have been about my size. That is to say, he must have been.

> (Beckett, 1980)

Using the language of democracy does not mean that writing lacks elegance or charm. Take, for example, this passage by the writer Iris Murdoch:

> The drawing room was full of golden firelight and there was a strong resinous smell of burning logs. The black-shaded lamps had been extinguished and the dark furry wallpaper glowed reddish and soft in the moving light. I saw at once and painfully that Palmer and Antonia were indeed not expecting us. They were sitting side by side in two upright chairs by the fire. Palmer had his arm around my wife and their faces, turned

tenderly towards each other were seen clearly in profile, each outlined with a pencil of gold. They seemed in that momentary vision of them like deities upon an Indian frieze, enthroned, inhumanly beautiful, a pair of sovereigns, distant and serene. They turned towards us, startled but not yet risen, still gracious in their arrested communion ...

(Murdoch, 1961)

A lawyer who respects history is more likely to write like Mellinkoff:

Fixed calendar time is the place to start. But calendar time fixed in a lease does not fix the durability of the relationship. A month-to-month lease, one either side could have ended in 30 days, frequently lasts for many years. With that sort of good feeling, on which a large proportion of business thrives, the short lease can be adjusted to suit the occasion. It need not be burdened from the start with the bric-a-brac typical of fixed long term duration. Simplicity may even encourage trust, and durability.

than like Bentham:

A law may be defined as an assemblage of signs declarative of a volition conceived or adopted by the sovereign in a state, concerning the conduct to be observed in a certain case by a certain person or class of persons, who in the case in question are or are supposed to be subject to his power: such volition trusting for its accomplishment to the expectation of certain events which it is intended such declaration should upon occasion be a means of bringing to pass, and the prospect of which it is intended should act as a motive upon those whose conduct is in question.

(From Bentham
Of Laws in General
in Lord LLoyd of Hampstead, 1977)

Simple words and simple structures convey meaning with speed and clarity. In a democratic society, lawyers have an important role but not an elevated one. Our language should reveal our ideas, not hide them.

Use of simple language has an additional benefit for the lawyer. If we try to use ordinary words in their ordinary meaning we will reveal meaning and relationships more clearly to ourselves during the thinking process. We shall then be able to convey both ideas and relationships between them more clearly to our readers.

6.3   Rule One: use ordinary words in their ordinary meaning

Where possible, try to use ordinary, workaday words which your reader can understand. Lawyers will always need to use special words with special meanings on occasion. Clarify when those limited occasions exist.

The corollary to this rule is you should not use ordinary words and ascribe special meanings. If you need to use a special word or phrase to do a special job, try to use a special word which is truly descriptive of your meaning.

When using ordinary words with their ordinary meanings remember that some words have a dual character; they are both ordinary words and law words. Take, for example, the word *contract*'. For the person in the street this means a *piece of paper*. For a lawyer, it is more likely to mean *the process of entering into an enforceable obligation through the process of offer and acceptance,* which might be represented by more than one piece of paper. If you use what to the non-lawyer appears to be a normal word, but in its specialist legal meaning, then you should say so.

Take, for example, the classic formulation of the test of reasonableness in negligence. The trier of fact is required to sit in the position of the defendant and to judge whether the defendant's behaviour falls short of what the reasonable man or woman would have done under the same circumstances.

The substitution of the reasonable man or woman defendant for the actual defendant is described as an *objective* test.

However, what is meant by *objective* in this context is not the ordinary meaning of the word.

An *objective* test is one that any person can apply and that will result in the same answer no matter who applies it. For example, the test *whether the beaker contains 500 millilitres of liquid* is an objective test.

Different judges or differently constituted juries asking themselves what a reasonable man or woman would do, on the other hand, might come to many different *objective* answers. This is not an objective test. It is instead an important device which aims to minimise (rather than eliminate) the impact of personal biases and prejudices.

It is not *objective* in the way in which this word is ordinarily understood.

6.4   Rule Two: use ordinary words, preferably one at a time

This rule has multiple facets.

6.4.1 A number of classes of legal words which could not be considered ordinary are excluded by virtue of this rule. The following is a section from Mellinkoff's definitive work on *The Language of the Law* (1963). These examples are used commonly in letters and memos.

- **Old and Middle English Words**

   Aforesaid, forthwith, henceforth, hitherto, moreover, thenceforth, therefore, thereto, whilst, whence, whensoever.

- **Old Formalisms**

   Respectfully submit, the undersigned, come on for hearing.

- **Law Latin**

   Inter alia (among others), mutatis mutandis (making the appropriate changes), re (in regard to).

- **Law French**

   Cestui que trust (beneficiary), demise (choose the appropriate word between death, lease, convey, conveyance), save (except), suffer (permit).

- **Law Argot**

  Argot is the colloquial language or slang of a profession or trade. A carpenter might talk about *a 4 by 2*, meaning a piece of wood four inches by two inches. Lawyers talk about a case being *on all fours* with another case (standing for the same point), *a matter* (a file or a case), *an inferior court* (a court which is not the last court of appeal), *a clog on the equity of redemption* (some act preventing the right to be exercised), or something being *otiose* (superfluous, useless) or being *rendered nugatory* (useless, trifling).

6.4.2 Lawyers not only use rare words, but also often use them in either pairs or triples; for example, *save and except, to have and to hold, give devise and bequeath, set aside and extinguish.*

Mellinkoff (1963) traces how these doubles and triples evolved. One example from the language of legal drafting reflects the change from Latin to Law French to English as the language of the law evolved; the expression *give, devise and bequeath.* Originally, one could dispose of personal chattels only, since land went to the first son under the rule of primogenitor; presumably it would have been the monks who made any note of a written *bequest*. The right to *devise* land was a limited right of gift which required a special term and a word was chosen which seems to have come from the Norman overlords. The general Anglo-Saxon *give* was added when the capacity to dispose of ones own property was extended to all property, but in careful lawyers' fashion the more specialised words were not dropped.

In Mellinkoff's later book (1982), a comprehensive list of these pairs or triples is given which he confidently states can be omitted with no loss of meaning. Many items in the list are expressions used in writing although some are more common in drafting. Some of the expressions to avoid in writing are *deem and consider, each and all, each and every, fit and proper, fit and suitable, goods and chattels, just and reasonable, null and void, about and concerning, part and parcel, void and of no effect.*

Sometimes, one legal word actually describes a concept which requires many words to explain. The example of the word *contract* has been given already. The use of these terms of art to make a succinct introductory statement can be useful, but be aware that sometimes you might need to explain.

> Some of the testimony was inadmissible as hearsay. This means that some of the sworn evidence was not permitted to be heard or taken into account by the jury because it was given second-hand - the witness was merely reporting what he had heard someone else say. That other person was not in the court to be cross-examined. Therefore, the judge decided that the jury should not consider these statements.

A term of art will be this type of handy succinct expression. The other kinds of legal words - argot and the various archaisms - are not terms of art.

6.4.3 The third element of this rule is that ordinary words should be used one at a time. You should avoid using expressions when one word will do. The following is a short list of commonly used wordy expressions and their substitutes.

would you be good enough to	please
we should be grateful if you would	please
we would ask that you	please
is predicated on the assumption that	assumes
in connection with	about
in relation to	about
in respect of	about
in the event of	if, when
with regard to	about

6.4.4 Perhaps there is a fourth element of this rule. George Orwell directed that a word of Anglo-Saxon origin be used in preference to one with a French, Latin or other derivation.

Following this rule, one would prefer *freedom* to *liberty*, *napkin* to *serviette*. Or as Churchill said,

> We must have a better word than *pre-fabricated*. Why not *ready-made*?
>
> Churchill
> *Closing the Ring*

Words of Anglo-Saxon origin tend to be shorter and more succinct. It is doubtful, though, whether this advice is of much use to the technical writer in an age in which *pre-fabricated* is already in common usage as the noun *pre-fab*. (Which, being short and ending in a consonant, is a word more Anglo-Saxon in appearance and sound.) Given the development of the European community and the place of English as a world language, it might be even kinder to use words of French or Latin origin which are shared by a number of cultures.

6.5   Rule Three: use inclusive, gender-neutral language

Our thinking can be limited by our language. Thus if we always represent successful actions as being attached to middle class, white, Anglo-Saxon, tertiary educated, heterosexual males, we are discriminating on the grounds of racism, gender and sexual preference. Express discrimination is more easily dealt with than unconscious discrimination. Good writing takes both the conscious and the unconscious into account. The rule that *the masculine includes the feminine* tries to represent language as neutral. The power of language in structuring our thinking and limiting or focusing our ideas is so great, that we must make an effort to move away from neutrality to conscious inclusiveness.

The unconscious expression of ideas expressed in male formulation is endemic in the legal profession, and male and female authors are equally responsible for perpetuating male-only forms. Sentences such as the following just trip off the pen:

- A client should ensure that his business operates on a sound footing.
- This rule applies to each company director who has an independent responsibility to ensure that the company does not trade while insolvent and pledges his assets to creditors accordingly.
- The applicant should complete this form in his handwriting.

These errors are easily remedied.

Use the definite article *the* instead of the pronoun *his*

A client should ensure that the business operates on a sound footing.

Express the idea in the plural

This rule applies to company directors who each have an independent responsibility to ensure that the company does not trade while insolvent and they pledge their assets to creditors accordingly.

Direct the idea to the reader using the you form

You should complete this form in your own handwriting.

A substitute for the you form is to say

The applicant should complete this form in his or her own writing.

On rare occasions it will be both necessary and desirable to underline the point that the direction or comment applies to both sexes. Use of this technique frequently, though, is too cumbersome for succinct expression.

These are the four techniques that I have consciously tried to adopt in this book.

Other techniques are used well in other contexts. Authors of parent help manuals (such as Penelope Leach) or dissertations on children's writing or painting, often adopt the expedient of referring to the child interchangeably as a *him* in one chapter and then as a *her* in the next. Such books also need to deal with issues of difference as well as issues of equality.

Substitute expressions denoting business or community roles with male words can usually be found

chairman	chairperson
	chair
	convener
	co-ordinator
craftsman	artisan
foreman	leader (of a jury)
handyman	maintenance worker
insurance man	repairer, maintenance worker
ombudsman	ombud, commissioner, protector
policemen	police
yachtsman	mariner

Where there is no adequate one word substitute, succinctness must give way to inclusiveness

| businessmen | business men and business women |
| salesmen | sales men and sales women |

6.6   Rule Four: delete intensifiers, qualifiers and other free-loading words

Lawyers generally quite like to reinforce their language with adjectives or adverbs that reduce or intensify meaning.

Many legal sentences can be improved by eliminating adjectives and adverbs. Take the first part of the last sentence. It drives home its meaning when the intensifiers and modifiers have been removed.

Lawyers like to reinforce their language with adjectives or adverbs that reduce or intensify meaning.

Sometimes, we use all the common intensifiers or qualifiers interchangeably with no discernible difference in meaning. For example, try to place in the sentence below as many of the words in this list - *generally, obviously, mostly, quite, particularly, apparently, critical, really*.

You can say,

Our clients are generally concerned about the really serious plight of the defendants in this particular class action.

With equal meaning you can say,

> Obviously our clients are particularly concerned about the apparently serious plight of the defendants in this class action.

Or you can say,

> Our clients are most concerned about the plight of the defendants in this really critical class action.

They all sound like platitudes!

The canny psychologist can draw some interesting conclusions when some of these unnecessary words pop up. For example, when a lawyer says *obviously* ..., it is certain that the idea expressed was a revelation to the writer at the time it was dictated. When a lawyer says *apparently* ..., it is usually because it was apparent to all the world years ago and the lawyer is just catching on. Lawyers use *quite* to modify implied criticism of their betters (as in *the judgment of his Lordship on this point was quite insistent*) or to damn the work of others with faint praise (as in *the research undertaken for this forty page advice memo was quite competent*). They always use the word *reasonable* in association with their own fees and disbursements, but the adjective *excessive* is often found when referring to the actions or the charges of the other side.

6.7   A postscript: language use when referring to documents and statutes

The above advice is relevant in writing letters, memos, briefs to Counsel or summaries of the law. Some of it can be applied to drafting. The advice to avoid archaic language and doubles and triples is easy when writing. When writing you are usually explaining or describing the law and what should be done about it, you are not purporting to create law or make rules as one does in drafting a contract, or lease or another legal document.

Sometimes when drafting it will be necessary to use archaic language irrespective of your own preferences for plain English. Sometimes the empowering statute will use an antique expression or wordy phrase. To substitute that for something expressed more plainly would run the risk that it would not be legally effective for the client.

For example, in one common law jurisdiction (Victoria, Australia), the form of the petition of a creditor to the Court to wind up a company which has not paid its debt to the petitioner is in the form of a *prayer* addressed to *This Honourable Court*.

But when you come to explain this clause to your client, you would not need to refer to the petition as a *prayer*. It would be normal to refer to it as an *application*.

This advice also applies when dealing with *shall* or *may* clauses. Suppose a lease provided for a list of more than twenty obligations of the tenant. The lease might say, for example, *The tenant shall pay the rent*. You could describe these obligations in more ordinary language as obligations of the tenant or things that the tenant must do. Thus you would not say,

> The lease provides that the tenant shall pay the rent, maintain the premises etc.

But you would say,

> The lease provides that you are to pay the rent, maintain the premises etc.

To adopt the formal language of the lease by way of explanation misunderstands the status of the letter of advice. A letter does not *create* law, it merely *explains* it. The Golden Rule (do not change your language if your meaning is unchanged) is not as important as the need to communicate to the client. The 'you' form and paraphrase in natural spoken language is more powerful and clearer.

Another good example of the unnecessary and misconceived use of legal forms is often seen in student assignments as well as in legal letters. It is neither appropriate nor necessary to say that you 'respectfully submit' in a letter or a memorandum when you disagree with some other lawyer's (or judge's) version of the law. Respectful submissions are the exclusive preserve of advocates when talking to judges.

6.8   From the particular to the general

The book so far has

- distinguished legal writing from other writing
- described lessons from artists and scientists which bear upon writing
- connected the process of writing with the process of thinking
- analysed things to do and things to avoid with paragraphs, sentences and words.

The next Chapter looks at the structures and patterns appropriate for the expression of legal ideas.

6.9   End of chapter references and additional reading

Beckett, S   *The End*
(1980)   from a collection of short stories
                     The Expelled and other novellas
                     Penguin Books Ltd

Bentham, J   *Of Laws in General*
                     quoted in Lord Lloyd of Hampstead 1977
                     Introduction to Jurisprudence
                     Steven & Sons

Mellinkoff, D   *The Language of the Law*
(1963)   Little Brown

Mellinkoff, D   *Legal Writing: Sense and Nonsense*
(1982)   West Publishing Company

Murdoch, I   *A Severed Head*
(1961)   1987 ed
                     Penguin Books Ltd

Public Record Office *Historical Records of Victoria,*
Victoria   *Foundation Series*
(1981)   *Beginnings of Permanent Government*
                     Volume One, ed Jones, P
                     Victoria Government Printing Office

CHAPTER

7 Logic, Structure and Patterns in Legal Writing

> *THEREFORE*
> *Three white lines*
> *joining exactly,*
> *all the angles equal.*
>
> Judith Wright

7.1 The importance of patterns

This wonderfully visual image of logical reasoning as a triangle actually refers to mathematics but is equally true of reasoning in law. Every piece you write will have an underlying pattern of reasoning which should be discernible to the reader. The pattern might be a chronology, or it might be an ordering of ideas based on importance, or identifying cause and effect. If the reader cannot discern your pattern early in the text, the reader will infer a pattern and draw conclusions from that inference. If the pattern you reveal is not the same as the one inferred, the reader becomes annoyed and confused.

For example, if a judge begins a judgment with the following sentences, where do you think they are leading?

On June 30, 1989, Mr James Sutherland booked a holiday to Surfer's Paradise on Australia's Gold Coast through Qantas. He had examined the travel brochures of ten travel companies to various destinations in the world before selecting this packaged tour. He packed very light clothes and three pairs of swimming trunks in anticipation of the warm weather. He took one business suit and his golf clubs. After three days in Surfer's Paradise his skin was so burnt that the doctor he saw advised him to stay off the beach for the remaining six days of his vacation. He purchased a product called Sunglow from the local pharmacist which gave remarkable relief.

If this were the beginning of a novel, these six sentences might be leading to a flashback to the whole of Mr Sutherland's life, or to a story about the people he met and the relationships he formed while staying indoors, or to a psychological crisis brought on from too much thought in idleness.

A legal context narrows the possibilities, but there are still many choices. Perhaps Mr Sutherland decided to buy a business and settle down in Australia but did not obtain the correct visa. Perhaps he is suing Qantas for representing that it was safe to frolic in the sun all day when this can in fact cause not only severe sunburn - as in Mr Sutherland's case - but also skin cancer. Perhaps Mr Sutherland met Miss Penelope Blenkinsop at a museum during those six days, married her in the heat of the moment and this judgment is about the property settlement following their acrimonious divorce.

We do not know the pattern the facts are supposed to form and therefore cannot concentrate on taking in all the facts. What relevance has the packing of the business suit? Why do we need to know that he chose his holiday from ten on offer? Why Australia as opposed to somewhere closer? What is the relevance of the sunburn?

Proper patterning of the ideas means that the reader will never need to ask why certain ideas are relevant at the time of reading. In art, ideas irrelevant to the narrative still might be relevant to the development of a character or of a mood in the work. Ambiguity and inference form part of the pattern. In business, on the other hand, the reader assumes that any idea noted in the text is there because it is relevant. Patterning involves two features:

- choosing a pattern
- revealing the pattern clearly to the reader.

Taking the simplest point first, advance organisation is normally the quickest and clearest way for business writers to reveal the pattern chosen to the reader.

7.2   Revealing the pattern: using advance organisation

Adapting the example above, the reader would not have questions about the relevance of the certain ideas, nor would the reader have been able to draw wrong inferences, if the paragraph had commenced:

> **In this case the Plaintiff is suing for damages for loss incurred by him in relying upon misrepresentations allegedly made to him during a brief trip to Australia on holiday when he purchased the licence for the product Sunglow for the territory of the United Kingdom.**
>
> **The facts are as follows.** On June 30, 1989, Mr James Sutherland booked a holiday to Surfer's Paradise on Australia's Gold Coast through Qantas. He had examined the travel brochures of ten travel companies to various destinations in the world before selecting this packaged tour. He packed very light clothes and three pairs of swimming trunks in anticipation of the warm weather. He took one business suit and his golf clubs. After three days in Surfer's Paradise his skin was so burnt that the doctor he saw advised him to stay off the beach for the remaining six days of his vacation. He purchased a cream called Sunglow from the local pharmacist which gave remarkable relief.

The sentences set out in bold prepare the reader for the context in which the information which follows is to be understood.

Advance organisation can be used at any level in the text; in the introduction to the text, in the introduction to a group of paragraphs, in the topic sentence of a paragraph or even as a form of summarising ideas in a sentence.

It can be used at the beginning of a text to tell the reader the questions to be dealt with and the topic order. Unless the reader is told, or unless the order is a completely familiar one to the reader, revealing the topics one at a time is a bit like a magician pulling coloured scarves at random out of a hat.

For example, advance organisation was used in the beginning of this Chapter to summarise patterning under two headings: choice of pattern and revealing that choice to the reader.

Advance organisation can also be used at the beginning of a section comprising several paragraphs. The sunburn narrative (above) is an example of this.

Advance organisation can also be used in a topic sentence to introduce the issues dealt with in a paragraph. The following extract from this book is an example of this. The topic sentence is set out in bold type.

> The conclusion? *Topic sentences assist both the writer and the reader.* The topic sentence assists the writer to check that the paragraph deals with the same subject-matter at the same level in the argument. The topic sentence assists the reader to concentrate at each staging point in the argument and to scan a work to find the only point of interest.
>
> (para 4.2.2)

Advance organisation can even be used to prepare the reader for the information to be conveyed in one sentence. At para 7.1 above, the following advance organisation was offered in this form:

> Patterning involves two features:
>
> • choosing a pattern
>
> • revealing the pattern clearly to the reader.

If I had chosen not to use this technique, I could have simply collapsed the ideas into a sentence structured as follows:

> Patterning involves choosing a pattern and revealing the pattern chosen clearly to the reader.

The sentence written without advance organisation is actually more elegant. However, it is more difficult to scan, harder to find the formulation of the points and requires the reader to work out that there are only two features.

Effective use of advance organisation means that the reader never meets anything new or unexpected in the body of the text because it will have been introduced previously at a higher level of generality.

7.3   Choosing a pattern

When asked to justify why ideas are ordered in a particular way, legal writers will inevitably say that the order is *logical*. Logic is in fact only one of four possible patterns. Time, structure and values are the other three orders. When lawyers say that an order is *logical*, they really mean *appropriate*. But for whom? The writer, or the reader?

The problem for legal writers is that we often think through a problem in the way that directors make feature films. The scene in which the main character dies might be shot before the scene in which the character is born. The right order will be restored in the editing room. Likewise, in thinking through a legal problem, we do not necessarily focus on issues chronologically, or even in order of importance. Perhaps what turns out to be a minor issue began as the only issue originally posed by the client. We dealt with that first and then the text grew around it.

For the reader, however, a minor issue should be mentioned later in the text. The major issues should be dealt with first.

There are a number of choices offered to the writer in patterning the relationships between ideas so that the reader understands where the writer is heading without diversion. The relationships between ideas will correspond to one or more of the following four patterns:

- logic
- time
- structure
- values.

7.4   Logic

The word logical is often used ambiguously by lawyers. It could be used to mean the use of the logical processes of deduction and induction, or it may simply mean that a particular structure or pattern used is, in the lawyer's view, appropriate. In this book, 'logic' means using the process of deduction and induction.

7.4.1 Deductive and inductive reasoning

Logic gives rise to two classic thinking patterns; deduction and induction.

The purpose of deductive reasoning is to apply a rule to a fact in life and to draw conclusions. The classic example in formal logic is the following:

Rule: All men are mortal

Life: Socrates is a man

Conclusion: Therefore, Socrates is mortal.

The purpose of deductive reasoning in law is to apply a fact in life to a rule in law and to draw conclusions, either about the legality of actions in the past or the permissibility of actions for the future. For example,

Rule: Company directors must be adults

Life: John is a minor seeking to be a company director

Conclusion: Therefore, John cannot be a company director.

Deductive reasoning requires a pre-existing rule. Inductive reasoning, on the other hand, requires the thinker to infer the rule from a number of facts in life. The most famous legal example is *Donoghue v Stevenson*. Set out simply, the process from that case is as follows:

1   The claim in *George v Skivington* by a plaintiff who was injured by a noxious hairwash was allowed even although the plaintiff had not purchased the hairwash.

2   The claim in *Langridge v Levy* by a plaintiff who was injured by a defective gun was allowed even though the plaintiff had not purchased the gun.

3   Therefore, the manufacturer of a bottle of gingerbeer will be liable to the person who consumed the gingerbeer and was injured because the bottle contained a partially decomposed snail even where the gingerbeer was purchased by a friend.

Rule inferred: (A) manufacturer of products, which he sells in such a form as to show that he intends them to reach the ultimate consumer in the form in which they left him with no reasonable possibility of intermediate examination, and with the knowledge that the absence of reasonable care in the preparation or putting up of the products will result in an injury to the consumer's life or property, owes a duty of care to the consumer to take that reasonable care.

(per Lord Atkin at page 599)

We also use inductive reasoning when we apply facts from life in a judgment in which the judge has not clearly formulated the ratio of the case. In order to do this we need to work out a statement of the rule for which the case stands (the ratio). Often the ratio is to be inferred from a combination of what the judge has said and the facts of the case.

We then use deductive reasoning when we apply our own facts from life to a rule thus inferred.

Deduction and induction are about thinking. What patterns should such thinking take when being communicated to a reader?

First, in formulating most arguments based on logic, ideas will naturally move from the most general to the most particular.

Second, whether using deduction or induction, the best order to communicate logical ideas will involve placing conclusions first.

7.4.2 Moving from the general to the particular

Taking the analogy of film-making a little further, imagine a director of a documentary who wishes to introduce a documentary about the life of villagers outside Calcutta. Such a documentary might start with a world map and move slowly to the hemisphere, country, nearest main city and location of the village. If the documentary started with a village scene, the viewer might assume that the film is about Bali or the Maldives or Madagascar when in fact it is about India. Starting off with the map means that the viewer need never adjust expectations.

Moving from the general to the particular means that you will state at the beginning of a text the topics that you will deal with at a high level of generality. Often an initial statement at a high level of generality is missing from legal text.

Example

Not

The case of **A. plc v Smith, Smith and Jones** was handed down by the Court of Appeal yesterday.

In that case the auditors had conducted an annual and an interim audit and in both cases had understated the company's creditors. A. plc purchased shares in the company. It then brought an action against the auditors in negligence claiming the difference between the price paid and the lesser value which would have been attributed to the shares if the creditors had been properly stated.

The Court held that there was no causal connection between the conduct of the auditors and the alleged loss. The directors had decided to make the purchase because of the substantial income accrued to the company which did not appear on the balance sheet. A. plc, therefore, was not entitled to any damages. This was in spite of the fact that the Court found that a duty of care was owed to future purchasers including A. plc and that the auditors had been negligent.

But

The case of **A. plc v Smith, Smith and Jones** was handed down by the Court of Appeal yesterday. **The Court considered the question of whether auditors owed a duty of care to a future purchaser of shares where creditors had been negligently understated in an audit** (general statement).

In that case the auditors had conducted an annual and an interim audit and on both occasions had understated the company's creditors. A. plc purchased shares in the company. It then brought an action against the auditors in negligence claiming the difference between the price paid and the lesser value which would have been attributed to the shares if the creditors had been properly stated.

The Court held that there was no causal connection between the conduct of the auditors and the alleged loss. The directors had decided to make the purchase because of the substantial income accrued to the company which did not appear on the balance sheet. A. plc, therefore, was not entitled to any damages. This was in spite of the fact that the Court found that a duty of care was owed to future purchasers including A. plc and that the auditors had been negligent (specific findings of the Court and reasoning).

This ordering also enables the reader to make correct inferences while the work is being read.

The order of topics within a document should also move from the general to the particular. Thus, for example, the lessee's covenants in a lease usually start with important provisions generally applicable such as payment of rent and finish with obligations applicable at some times only, such as compliance with local authority notices.

7.4.3 Conclusions first

Deductive and inductive logic are thinking patterns. In practical terms you do not need to be aware of whether you are using induction or deduction because patterning in writing is about selecting **communication** patterns for the reader. In logical argument, you will need to work hard to make sure that the reader does not jump ahead and make false inferences from your expression of the facts and the rules. You can do this by placing conclusions first. If you place your conclusions first, the reader will not be tempted to infer other conclusions which then prove to be false.

There is a secondary reason for placing conclusions first. Clients often seek legal advice in the form of answers to questions. Not all the questions asked imply logical processes for answering. When they do, it is easier for the reader to understand the tenor of the argument if the answer is given immediately after the question and before the explanation. It is probable that experienced business readers hunt for the answer before reading the explanation because the answer will tell them what should be done. Therefore, why not place the ideas in the order most helpful to the reader?

7.4.4 Communication patterns for logical argument: a summary

An appropriate communication pattern for the presentation of logical argument is one in which

1 ideas move from the general to the particular

2 conclusions are presented before arguments or explanations at each stage.

The technique of advance organisation (see para 7.2 above) and the two logical communication patterns of general to particular and conclusions first, can be used together as a kind of mutual support system for the text. You may like to think of the principle of advance organisation as an external skeleton supporting ideas. By definition, if you organise ideas in advance then you will be telling the reader what the text will contain and how the text will be organised. On the other hand the principles of general to particular and conclusions first are internal skeletons. They help build a pattern which will be discernible to the reader by implication rather than express statement.

7.5   Time

Time is another pattern which can be used to glue together ideas. You may narrate a past experience in **chronological order**. Chronology may also be appropriate if you are designating procedures for another person to follow.

Cause and effect is another time pattern. If causation is the issue, then you might be using a variation of time order by starting with the effects and then examining causes. Or, if you are analysing whether a client can achieve certain objectives by taking certain actions in the future, then you might begin by stating the objectives ('cause') and then proceed to an examination of proposed actions ('effect').

7.6 Structural patterns

Structural patterns are very common in law. Life constantly seems to throw up similar problems for legal resolution. Lawyers have developed a kind of protocol about how they tackle the given explanation. You use a structural pattern every time you decide to discuss a legal problem in a sequence already set out in a document or common in a particular legal subject. For example, contracts are often discussed through the sequence offer and acceptance to discharge and remedies. The structural pattern of contract is itself based on a chronological process of entering into a contract.

The ordering of problem-solving often taught in law school - to set out the facts, identify issues, apply the facts to the law and then advise - is itself a structural order.

Many lawyers would call both structural and time orders 'logical'. What they actually mean is 'appropriate' (see para 7.4 above).

7.7 Value patterns

Sometimes you will pattern information according to the values of your client. You might propose solutions in the order from the cheapest to the most expensive. You might set out to discuss client concerns by moving from the issue of greatest importance to the client to those of least importance. If you need to discuss a whole contract you might use a structural order; offer, acceptance and so on. But if you need to discuss one aspect only of a contract (perhaps methods of discharge) you might substitute the traditional structural order for values order; for example, setting out for your client the most to the least efficacious methods of discharge.

7.8   Law ideas and life ideas: how the patterns combine

Some writers have difficulty with the concept of patterns because at any one time you might be using all four patterns, or only one.

Each pattern overlaps with the other three and helps to construct and to support the argument. You might like to think of an author as being like a printer who prints a colour document four times, each time with a different colour in order to create the final recognisable image.

Fortunately, in legal writing there are some common combinations of patterns. It may help you to conceptualise these combinations if you think about the subject-matter of legal writing under two headings only: life and law.

In life, time and value patterns will be most important. You will need to set out the facts in chronological order. The client's concerns and recommendations for action will often be clearest expressed in a value pattern.

In law, logical and structural patterns will be most important in discussion of the law and in the application of the law to the facts. Chronological patterns will become important when talking about who should do what, when and how. Values patterns will become important in making recommendations which are persuasive.

A letter of legal advice commonly follows the structural pattern:

- reader's beginning
- statement of issues
- statement of facts
- explanation of law
- application of law to facts
- making recommendations.

Within this structural pattern, the topics might combine as follows.

The **reader's beginning** will use advance organisation by telling the reader which questions will be discussed.

If there is more than one issue, **the statement of issues** might be ordered in a **values pattern** (from most to least important) or in a **time pattern** (from the question of most urgency to that of least urgency).

The statement of facts would normally use a chronological pattern moving from the past to the present.

The explanation of law might use several patterns. Overall, the legal issues to be explained might adopt **a values pattern** (most to least important to the client). Each issue might move in a **logical order**, putting conclusions first and discussing the law from the general to the specific (for example, rule first, examples next, exceptions next, examples of exceptions next).

The **application of law to the facts** might involve more than one interpretation. A **values order** moving down from that considered most likely to be correct will often be appropriate.

Conclusions will normally have been mentioned in the explanation of the law but they need to be translated into **recommendations for action.** This might involve several patterns. First, you might list recommendations in the order in which the issue was discussed in the text (structural order). You might then specifically re-order them into values order (eg fastest to slowest, cheapest to most expensive). You might then re-order them further by using **time order** for the steps within each recommendation to be taken and by whom.

7.9   Conclusion

Patterning is the most abstract concept in writing. It asks you to make conscious decisions about matters formerly based on instinct. Patterning asks you to abandon the order of thought and substitute for it an order of clear communication. It asks you to help the reader understand the questions you have posed, the answers and the reasons to form a path for the reader from the questions to the answers. Patterning for the reader requires you to choose a series of patterns suitable for the explanation, *not* to describe your thought processes while you were wrestling with the questions.

CHAPTER

8 Turning Advice into Action

8.1 The relative importance of plain language and clear patterns

Legal language is of great concern to people in the community, yet reader tests have shown (Eagleson, 1986) that archaic words are not always a bar to comprehension. Readers are often able to understand the gist of what is meant if the structure is right. This suggests that when revising you should apply the guidelines given in this book about structuring paragraphs, sentences and ideas first and later focus on language.

Why might you need to make this choice? After one, even very thorough, reading of this and other books on legal writing, you will not recall everything. You will need to focus your quest for self-improvement over time; mastering a few items and then moving on. In order to increase your recall of things to avoid and characteristics to strive for, you will need to focus your quest for self-improvement either on structure or on language.

Remember the Writ of Attachment in Chapter Six? The relationship between structure and language can be illustrated by taking another look at this example. First, re-punctuate the Writ of Attachment using shorter sentences and then try arranging the ideas better. The original text is given first below as a reminder.

Original text

> Elizabeth the Second, by the Grace of God Queen of Australia and all Her other Realms and Territories, Head of the Commonwealth,
>
> To the Sheriff, Greeting:
>
> We command you to attach [the Defendant] , so as to have him before us in our Supreme Court, there to answer us, as well touching a contempt which he it is alleged hath committed against us, as also such other matters as shall be then and there laid to his charge, and further to perform and abide such order as our said Court shall make in this behalf; and hereof, fail not, and bring this writ with you.

Re-punctuated text

WRIT

From: Queen Elizabeth the Second etc
To: The Sheriff of the Supreme Court
And to: The Defendant

We command you to attach the Defendant and bring him to the Supreme Court to answer a charge of contempt. It is alleged that he hath made a contempt and such other matters against us as might be laid to his charge then and there. You are also to abide and perform such further orders that the Court shall make in this behalf and to perform these tasks dutifully. You are commanded to bring this writ with you.

Re-punctuating this example clarifies meaning immediately. There are still a number of expressions in the text which use archaic language, but probably these no longer obscure the meaning.

Tabulation coupled with some minor changes will make it even clearer.

Tabulated version

WRIT

From: Queen Elizabeth the Second
To: The Sheriff of the Supreme Court
And to: The Defendant

We command you to:

1 Attach the Defendant and bring him to the Supreme Court to answer a charge of contempt which it is alleged he hath made against us and such other matters as may be laid to his charge there and then.

2 Abide and perform such other orders that the court shall make in this behalf.

3 Bring this Writ with you.

4 Perform these task dutifully.

The original text was a set of directions placed more or less in action order. The re-written versions highlight the action order and make the text easier to scan and refer back to. The tabulated version highlights the time order.

Where the original text contains ideas which are already expressed using clear language and there is little time for revision, shortening sentences, co-ordinating expressions in longer sentences and providing tabulation will result in a big improvement for a small investment of time. This exercise will also reveal if the underlying pattern of ideas suggests that their expression could be better organised (see Chapter Seven).

8.2   When to revise language first

Remember the extract from Jeremy Bentham in Chapter Six? It presents a different problem. No doubt it was written for a highly specialised audience of scholars. The ideas, however, are not very clearly expressed because some of the words used to express main concepts are unclear. Even by re-punctuating the lay reader will not get far with the meaning.

Original text

A law may be defined as an assemblage of signs declarative of a volition conceived or adopted by the sovereign in a state, concerning the conduct to be observed in a certain case by a certain person or class of persons, who in the case in question are or are supposed to be subject to his power: such volition trusting for its accomplishment to the expectation of certain events which it is intended such declaration should upon occasion be a means of bringing to pass, and the prospect of which it is intended should act as a motive upon those whose conduct is in question.

Re-punctuated text

A law may be defined as an assemblage of signs declarative of a volition conceived or adopted by the sovereign in a state.

It concerns the conduct to be observed in a certain case by a certain person or class of persons, who, in the case in question, are or are supposed to be subject to the sovereign's power. Such volition trusts for its accomplishment to the expectation of certain events which it is intended such declaration should upon occasion be a means of bringing to pass, and the prospect of which it is intended should act as a motive upon those whose conduct is in question.

The re-punctuated text is easier to read. The meaning, though, is not much clearer because some of the expressions still have uncertain ambit. This is a case for revision of language first.

You will not have unlimited time for revision. Sometimes you will need to spend all your available time sharpening the ideas through your choice of language. You will then have less or no time in which to refine the structure. If you are writing for an audience who knows as much or more than you that will not matter so much. Where the ideas are already expressed in clear language, but the underlying patterns are not clear, you will be able to improve the communication of them to the reader by adopting some of the ideas about sentence and paragraph structure and patterning of ideas contained in this book.

8.3   Summary: when to focus on language

You will need to pay careful attention to the words used when you are

- formulating the problem statement
- narrating or confirming the facts
- making a transition between one part of the argument and another part
- defining legal rules
- stating the conclusion and recommendations.

These particular steps in legal writing require you to focus closely on the words used in a relatively small number of sentences. You will need the advice given in Chapter Six for this. You might also need to refer to the advice given in Chapter Five on sentence structure so that the words that carry the meaning are not flooded by prepositions, conjunctions, adjectives or adverbs.

8.4   Summary: when to focus on structure and patterns

You will be rewarded by paying careful attention to structure and patterns of ideas when you are

- ordering the sections of the text overall
- narrating facts or objectives
- sequencing rules
- applying facts to rules
- stating what should be done in what order.

For these steps in the process of legal writing, you should refer to the advice given in Chapters Four and Seven. This will require you to take a broader view of paragraph and sentence arrangement.

8.5   Three weeks or seven steps to better writing

Better writing will result from clearer and more confident thinking. When you can express your ideas clearly to yourself, you will find that fuzzy words and snaky sentences do not enter your prose. Your legal writing might need some refinement to convey the ideas to a reader on a first reading, but revision will not be a major task.

Many legal writers will find that much of their work is more like the Bentham text (para 8.2 above) than the Writ (para 8.1 above). It needs more thinking and less writing. I think of this as the big picture approach. It is the approach of the painter who prepares an outline of the picture and then paints in the picture section by section. I have set this approach out in a weekly routine which changes every week for three weeks. By the end of three weeks both your thinking and your writing will be clearer as a result. This approach focuses on structure and patterns. The language improvements tend to suggest themselves.

Alternatively, if the majority of your work is more like the Writ of Attachment, then a second approach, outlined below, will help you. It sets out a system for examining structure, patterns and language in more detail. I think of this as the small picture approach. It is the approach of the painter who paints a quadrant of the canvass in great detail before moving on to the next section. I have set this out in a seven step routine to be applied to selected pieces of writing.

Both approaches described below assume that you will start with a first draft and that you have word-processing facilities to prepare subsequent improvements.

Students, on the other hand, who produce occasional big event pieces, might find the seven step approach useful.

A word of warning. Using these routines is like going on a diet or giving up smoking. You will need both discipline and support to stick with it. Try setting up an obligation to report to someone on how you are getting on. Take copies from this book and place them on your pinboard so that they accuse you. Add to the pinboard samples of work you find embarrassing or which you believe consumed far too much time. Remember, this is war on bad writing and unclear thinking.

8.6   Three weeks to better writing

This approach is illustrated below by reference to an innocuous letter of advice written after a first meeting with the directors of a company which owns a small three storey building leased to another company as tenant. This is the first letter on file summarising the initial instruction-taking meeting.

Dear Sir,

I refer to your meeting with me on March 19.

You instruct that the lessee company rarely paid the rent on time as almost invariably the cheques were dated the 28th or 29th of the month when the due date was the 27th. The tenants also breached the lease by paying insurances required by clauses 7.2 and 7.3 late and failing to send you the certificates.

Furthermore, after a complaint about an electrical fault, your own electrician reported that the cable had been eaten by mice who appear to have been attracted by a kitchen kept in less than wholesome order. During two years of the lease the lessee company failed to pay the local authority taxes. A wall in the kitchen on the second floor was also so affected by the steam rising from the water heater which was installed by the lessee company after seeking your consent but was not fitted with the steam outlet in accordance with specifications shown to you, that the damp has now become a structural fault on the north wall of the whole building.

The estate agent managing the lease for you has sent a number of notices directing the tenants to comply with the provisions of the lease, but these have been ignored. You have instructed that legal fees and penalty interest are also now owing in respect of these notices.

Please let me know about any other breaches of the lease. You should feel free to amend or add to any of the breaches listed above. Once the list of breaches has been settled I can proceed to issue the requisite repairs notices and to prepare a letter of demand for the money outstanding.

You also think that the tenant might want to exercise an option to renew or to assign the lease to a third party.

If you have any questions, please do not hesitate to contact me. In the meantime, I look forward to your instructions about any amendments or additions you might have to a list of the breaches by the tenant.

Yours sincerely,

Janet Hazlehurst

8.6.1 Week One: focus on problem and conclusion

In my experience, this letter is representative of first letters seen on files all the time. The underlying fact pattern is quite simple. Undoubtedly both the author and the recipient know what is meant and what should be done in a general sort of way.

The problem is that this initial draft is a narrative of what was discussed in the meeting between the solicitor and the client. It is a mirror of the meeting and of the author's thought patterns. A letter advising on a legal problem should not be a mirror of what was said; rather, it should act as a centrifuge separating relevant and irrelevant facts. Then it should act as a decision tree structuring facts and legal issues into action-sequenced options for the client.

Even from the point of view of the needs of the several audiences who might need to use the letter, it has a number of flaws. **Another lawyer** picking up the file at that point would not be fully informed by reading the letter. What does the client wish to achieve? **The client company** is informed of its general rights, but has not been given choices about what should be done.

In this first week, you can improve letters of this type by asking yourself five simple questions. These are the five questions that busy partners who are asked to sign many letters a day tend to focus on in determining if anything really needs to go back for amendment. In my experience, when these five questions are asked, definite improvements can be made in about one-third of internal memos and in a higher proportion of client letters of advice.

1 Is the law right?

2 Has the letter begun at the reader's beginning?

3 Are the problems to be solved set out, preferably in question form?

4 Does the conclusion match the statement of the problem without raising more problems?

5 Does the recipient know what is to be done next and by whom?

1   Is the law right?

Without reading the lease, looking at the documentary evidence and listening to the client, it is difficult to be definitive, but the long list of apparent breaches would seem to justify this conclusion.

2   Has the letter begun at the reader's beginning?

No. The context needs to be inferred. The address of the property is omitted. It is clear that the landlord company contacted the lawyer but in what context? In the context of a recent breach (such as the discovery of the rising damp) or in the context of a request by the tenant company to assign the lease to a third party, or to exercise an option to extend the lease?

Context informs all other audiences about likely client expectations and objectives.

3   Are the problems to be solved stated, preferably in question form?

No. We can infer generally that the landlord is not happy with the tenant's breaches. It would appear that the client might also want advice on what could be done if the tenant applies to exercise an option to renew the lease or to assign the lease to a third party. These are just stated as facts rather than as legal issues. Most landlords would need to know if the facts giving rise to breaches might entitle the landlord to refuse to assign or to consent to a further term or, if the breaches are serious, persistent and not rectified if the lease can be terminated.

4   Does the conclusion match the statement of the problem without raising more problems?

To some extent. However, the difficulty is that the conclusion is not very conclusive. It is as though the lawyers expect that the client might add to or amend the list of facts which contain possible breaches so significantly that decisions about what could be done need to be postponed. A really competent initial letter of advice will set up overall patterns for analysis and for action. The patterns can be added to or modified along the way but the lawyer who sets up such an initial pattern will be in control of the matter instead of the matter being in control of him or her.

5 Does the recipient know what is to be done next and by whom?

Yes, in a small way. The recipient is to confirm or to amend facts. The more important questions of possible action to be taken in relation to the lease in the event of requested assignment, lease renewal or persistent breach are left unanswered.

These questions require only amendment of the first and the last paragraphs. I have made up the necessary supplementary information. The amendments to the letter are set out in bold.

After Week One
Second Attempt

Dear Sir,

I refer to your meeting with me on March 19.

You are concerned that the tenant of your premises at 43 High Street has damaged the north wall of the building through a failure to ventilate a water heater adequately. This is merely the most recent example of many breaches since the tenant took possession. You would like to ensure that the tenant pays for the repairs to the wall and to recover other outstanding amounts.

You instruct that the lessee company rarely paid the rent on time as almost invariably the cheques were dated the 28th or 29th of the month when the due date was the 27th. The tenants also breached the lease by paying insurances required by clauses 7.2 and 7.3 late and failing to send you the certificates.

Furthermore, after a complaint about an electrical fault, your own electrician reported that the cable had been eaten by mice who appear to have been attracted by a kitchen kept in less than wholesome order. During two years of the lease the lessee company failed to pay the local authority taxes. A wall in the kitchen on the second floor was also so affected by the steam rising from the water heater which was installed by the lessee company after seeking your consent but was not fitted with the steam outlet in accordance with specifications shown to you, that the damp has now become a structural fault on the north wall of the whole building.

The estate agent managing the lease for you has sent a number of notices directing the tenants to comply with the provisions of the lease, but these have been ignored. You have instructed that legal fees and penalty interest are also now owing in respect of these notices.

Please let me know about any other breaches of the lease. You should feel free to amend or add to any of the breaches listed above. Once the list of breaches has been settled we can proceed to issue the requisite repairs notices and to prepare a letter of demand for the money outstanding.

Three other questions arise for consideration. First, would you be permitted to withhold your consent to an assignment of lease? If the breaches remain, yes. Second, could you resist an application by the tenant to exercise the option to renew or to extend the lease? If the breaches remain on foot, the answer is clearly, yes. Third, can you terminate the lease because of these breaches? Again, I think that the answer is yes.

These issues are slightly premature at this point, but you might want to give them some thought. In the meantime, I look forward to your instructions about any amendments or additions you might have to a list of the breaches by the tenant.

Yours sincerely,

Janet Hazlehurst

8.6.2 Week Two: pattern and patterning

By week two you will have made sure that all letters of advice give advice correct in law, state the context, the problem, the solution and who is to do what next (see above at para 8.6.1). You think that the amended version of the letter given above is a great improvement.

Now you can scrutinise the letter for patterning and to ask yourself the following questions:

1 Does the letter follow a clear overall pattern moving from the general to the particular?

2 Are there clear transitions between each of the patterns which are advance organised?

3 Are sections and sub-sections patterned appropriately?

1   Does the letter follow a clear overall pattern moving from the general to the particular?

The sequence is reasonably clear, but may be less so to a reader who is not a lawyer.

The letter follows the sequence often recommended at law school. It

- identifies the general problem
- sets out the facts
- applies the facts to the law
- makes recommendations.

Once we arrive at the narration of the facts, though, the sequence is like a thriller novel. The reader does not know when the narration of the facts will end. There is a great temptation for the client to move to the end of even this short letter in order to find the questions and the solutions.

The reporting of the facts is often tedious. The client will always see that as uninformative repetition. From the client's point of view it is important to set out the questions to be solved with conclusions *first.* Then the client knows how to judge the narration that follows.

Sometimes the matter is too complex or difficult to set out the answers at the outset, and even a summary of the answers is impossible. Then the author needs to make sure that the answers, where given, match the questions entirely.

Note also here that patterns can be made even clearer by the use of headings and sub-headings.

2   Are there clear transitions between each of the patterns which are advance organised?

Not always. The descent into the detail of the breaches should be prefaced by a general sentence introducing this topic. If you dislike the use of headings and sub-headings on stylistic grounds, then transitions will be particularly important.

3   Are sections and sub-sections patterned appropriately?

In a longer document, this would require you to look at the patterns of information in the letter overall, in each section and each sub-section. In this case, the actions of the managing agent in sending a notice should be brought closer to the front of the letter, because the failure to comply with the notices has now compounded the client's problems with the tenant.

The paragraphs about facts could pattern ideas better. First the breaches need to be classified and grouped in accordance with the classification. Some are financial breaches, some are building use breaches. The most current building use breach is the water heater which should be discussed first. Perhaps other building use breaches can be discussed second. (This would be patterning the building use breaches on a values pattern - ordering them from the breach of greatest concern through to least concern to the client.) Then financial breaches in chronological order.

The amendments have been set out in bold below.

After Week Two
Third Attempt

Dear Sir,

I refer to your meeting with me on March 19.

Your problem

You are concerned that the tenant of your premises at 43 High Street has damaged the north wall of the building through a failure to ventilate a water heater adequately. This is merely the most recent example of many breaches since the tenant took possession. You would like to ensure that the tenant pays for the repairs to the wall and to recover other outstanding amounts.

What you have done so far

The estate agent managing the lease for you has sent a number of notices directing the tenants to comply with the provisions of the lease, but these have been ignored. You have instructed that legal fees and penalty interest are also now owing in respect of these notices.

Legal Issues

Four broad questions arise for consideration. First, would you be permitted to withhold your consent to an assignment of lease? If the breaches remain, yes. Second, could you resist an application by the tenant to exercise the option to renew or to extend the lease? If the breaches remain on foot, the answer is clearly, yes. Third, can you terminate the lease because of these breaches? Again, I think that the answer is yes. Fourth, can you require the tenant to rectify the damage cause by the breaches and to pay outstanding amounts? The answer is, yes.

Tenant's breaches

There are three classes of breach under the lease: structural damage to the premises, other contraventions of building use and financial breaches.

A wall in the kitchen on the second floor was also so affected by the steam rising from the water heater which was installed by the lessee company after seeking your consent but was not fitted with the steam outlet in accordance with specifications shown to you, that the damp has now become a structural fault on the north wall of the whole building.

Furthermore, after a complaint about an electrical fault, your own electrician reported that the cable had been eaten by mice who appear to have been attracted by a kitchen kept in less than wholesome order.

We are instructed that the lessee company rarely paid the rent on time as almost invariably the cheques were dated the 28th or 29th of the month when the due date was the 27th. During two years of the lease the lessee company failed to pay the local authority taxes. The tenants also breached the lease by paying insurances required by clauses 7.2 and 7.3 late and failing to send you the certificates.

What you should do now

Please let us know about any other breaches of the lease. You should feel free to amend or add to any of the breaches listed above. Once the list of breaches has been settled, we can proceed to issue the requisite repairs notices and to issue a letter of demand for the money outstanding.

The three broader questions are as yet a little premature. You might like to give some thought to them so that if the tenant fails to comply with future demands, you have decided what you wish to do.

Yours sincerely,

Janet Hazlehurst

8.6.3 Week Three: paragraphs and sentences

Finally, re-read the letter and ask yourself the following questions:

1 Are there short sentences in introductions, transitions and conclusions with headings used to aid scanning?

2 Does each paragraph begin with a topic sentence?

3 Do the paragraphs have visual appeal?

Weeks one and two have produced a letter which has much better focus and clearer patterning of information. The focus on advance organisation means that the patterns have been revealed to the reader. The sole improvement required now is to make the letter easier to scan by introducing some sub-headings and by setting out the categories of breach more clearly.

The amendments have been set out in bold below.

After Week Three
Fourth Attempt

Dear Sir,

I refer to your meeting with me on March 19.

Your problem

You are concerned that the tenant of your premises at 43 High Street has damaged the north wall of the building through a failure to ventilate a water heater.adequately. This is merely the most recent example of many breaches since the tenant took possession. You would like to force the tenant to pay for the repairs to the wall and to recover other outstanding amounts.

What you have done so far

The estate agent managing the lease for you has sent a number of notices directing the tenants to comply with the provisions of the lease, but these have been ignored. You have instructed us that legal fees and penalty interest are also now owing in respect of these notices.

Legal issues

Four broad questions arise for consideration.

1   Would you be permitted to withhold your consent to an assignment of lease? If the breaches continue, yes.

2   Could you resist an application by the tenant to exercise the option to renew or to extend the lease? If the breaches continue, yes.

3   Can you terminate the lease because of these breaches? Again, I think that the answer is yes.

4   Can you require the tenant to rectify the damage cause by the breaches and to pay outstanding amounts? Yes.

How has the tenant breached the lease?

There are three classes of breach under the lease: structural damage to the premises, contraventions of building use and financial breaches.

Structural damage: A wall in the kitchen on the second floor was also so affected by the steam rising from the water heater which was installed by the lessee company after seeking your consent but was not fitted with the steam outlet in accordance with specifications shown to you, that the damp has now become a structural fault on the north wall of the whole building.

Contraventions of use: Furthermore, after a complaint about an electrical fault, your own electrician reported that the cable had been eaten by mice who appear to have been attracted by a kitchen kept in less than wholesome order.

Financial breaches: We are instructed that the lessee company rarely paid the rent on time as almost invariably the cheques were dated the 28th or 29th of the month when the due date was the 27th. During two years of the lease the lessee company failed to pay the local authority taxes. The tenants also breached the lease by paying insurances required by clauses 7.2 and 7.3 late and failing to send you the certificates.

What you should do now

Please let us know about any other breaches of the lease. You should feel free to amend or add to any of the breaches listed above. Once the list of breaches has been settled, we can proceed to issue the requisite repairs notices and to issue a letter of demand for the money outstanding.

The three broader questions are as yet a little premature. You might like to give some thought to them so that if the tenant fails to comply with future demands, you will be in a position to decide what you wish to do.

Yours sincerely,

Janet Hazlehurst

8.6.4 Three weeks to better writing: a summary

The week-by-week revision guidelines are summarised below. They could be incorporated into your review of letter drafts on a week-to-week basis, allowing you to concentrate on a different checklist for each letter in draft which comes across your desk. Sometimes an urgent time-frame may require you to go through this entire revision process in half a day; on other occasions you may be able to take more time between drafts.

Week One: focus on problem and conclusion

1.1 Is the law right?

1.2 Has the letter begun at the reader's beginning?

1.3 Are the problems to be solved set out preferably in question form?

1.4 Does the conclusion match the statement of the problem without raising more problems?

1.5 Does the recipient know what is to be done next and by whom?

Week Two: pattern and patterning

2.1 Does the letter follow a clear overall pattern moving from the general to the particular?

2.2 Are there clear transitions between each of the patterns which are advance organised?

2.3 Are sections and sub-sections patterned appropriately?

Week Three: paragraphs and sentences

3.1 Are there short sentences in introductions, transitions and conclusions with headings used to aid scanning?

3.2 Does each paragraph begin with a topic sentence?

3.3 Do the paragraphs have visual appeal?

8.7   Seven steps after three weeks

If you are a practitioner who writes volumes daily, you might need to run through the three week routine a few times before you have reached the stage at which you can prepare an outline before a first draft and can ensure that the final resembles the outline in pattern. At this point the seven step routine described below may prove to be a useful checklist for you. If you are a student trying to improve your essays or answers to problems, or someone who produces an occasional 'big event' piece, you might have the time and energy to follow the seven step routine on each piece of work.

It is seven steps, but it may not require reading the work seven times. If you find it hard to keep all these items in your head at once, then seven readings might be required. More experienced revisors will be able to revise in two sittings. Most people cannot read for content, correctness, style and proof-reading in one sitting. I proof-read and then read for content, correctness and style simultaneously in another sitting.

8.7.1 The seven step guide to revising

1 The solution and the facts relied upon should be correct

Check for conformity to your instructions and correctness in law.

2 The solution must match the statement of the problem

You should have answered all the questions posed by the client and raised no others which are left unanswered. This also involves a check to see that you have explained basic concepts following the Golden Rule - using language which is consistent, concrete and active.

3 Begin at the reader's beginning

For the introduction, check that you have made a transition for the reader by referring to what the reader knows already and then moving to the issues that you will deal with.

4 Overall patterns and patterns within sections and sub-sections

- Is each introduction and transition advance organised?
- Identify the underlying rationale for patterning of information overall, and in each section and sub-section. Is the underlying rationale
  - logic (moving from the general to the particular, with conclusions first)
  - time (eg chronology, cause-effect)
  - values (eg most to least recommended, most to least expensive)
  - structure (eg common legal order, following a document).

5   Features of each paragraph

- Check whether the paragraph is introductory, supporting, transitional or concluding.
- Check that the paragraph
  - begins with a topic sentence
  - has unity of content
  - has visual appeal
  - if a subordinate structure, moves from the general to the particular
  - if a co-ordinate structure, uses parallel and co-ordinate expressions.

6   Features of each sentences

For each sentence check that it

- only contains one idea
- is not ambiguous
- uses simple, clear, concrete, inclusive, active language
- mostly is in the order subject + verb + object
- avoids wordy expressions and archaisms
- is grammatically correct.

7   Typos and omissions

Read separately for common typographical errors (typos) and typing errors or omissions affecting meaning. Read the parts you agonised over the most, remembering Bradley's law (which states that typos and omissions cluster where there is greatest doubt).

8.8   Reducing the number of drafts by using an outline

If you are able to stick to either the three week routine for three weeks or to the seven step routine for several major pieces of work, you will find that you will be rewarded by producing progressively clearer first drafts.

After accomplishing some improvement through revision, you might then like to try to outline your work before producing a first draft and subjecting it to the seven step routine. You can reduce the number of drafts if you discipline yourself to produce an outline, a first draft and thereafter only a final. Think of this as exercise to tone the muscles like aerobics or swimming after you have lost all that weight.

8.9   How to outline

(See also Chapter Three para 3.2)

1   Brainstorm and list

Write in random order a list of the concepts that need to be dealt with and the questions which need to be answered. Settle on the basic vocabulary: how you will refer to the parties, which terms of art need to be used and explained.

2   Problem and recommendation

Write down a problem statement in language which is simple, clear, concrete and active. If you can, write down your conclusions and recommendations next to the problem. You might have to go through the next steps, though, and do this last.

3   Re-order your list

Decide the topics that need to be dealt with from your random list and the ways in which you will sequence the information. I do this by giving each section and sub-section a notional heading, whether I am going to use headings in the text or not. Each section and sub-section should contain no more than 7 items. Each sub-section should be capable of being dealt with in fewer than 7 paragraphs.

4 Recommendation

Complete your problem statement by writing your recommendation which you should have had time to conclude at the sub-conscious level through dealing with order. If you noted them at the time of noting the problem, check that they are correct now.

You might need to spiral around these steps several times before you have the problem statement, recommendation and topics for discussion in appropriate order. You should not really do a first draft until you have made decisions about these and have decided upon an answer.

8.10 Conclusion: how improving your writing will improve your thinking

In his wonderful book contemplating mathematics, music, art and computers, Douglas Hofstadter tells us that improvements in the design of computer programs have only been possible by

- improvements in computer **language**

- improvements in the way information is **patterned**.

(Hofstadter, 1979)

We can improve the clarity and force of legal expression by using as little technical language as possible so that when it is used, it clarifies reasoning rather than obscuring it.

We can improve the clarity of our own thinking by looking for patterns to convey ideas.

We can improve the clarity of legal expression by choosing patterns which will convey the ideas clearly to a particular reader.

These are the processes recommended in this book. You will know when your improved writing has clarified your thinking. It will be noticeable every time you decide to omit a concept, every time you move a conclusion to the top of an argument, every time you place yet another full stop. When you routinely produce clear, comprehensible and correct advice in one draft, you will know that it is not just an improvement in writing; you will have saved time and will have experienced great satisfaction with the improvement in your level of skill.

8.11   End of chapter references and additional reading

Eagleson, R   *Discussion Paper Number 1*
(1986)   Report of the Law Reform Commission
                               of Victoria

Hofstadter, D   *Goedel Escher and Bach:*
(1979)   *The Eternal Golden Braid*
                               Penguin Books Ltd

Appendix

A Benchmark Exercises

Managing Paragraphs

1   Identify the topic sentences in the following paragraphs:

(1) 'Office telephones are meant to be used for office purposes. Using them privately without consent is essentially no different from taking someone else's money without consent. Even more important, if lines are blocked by private telephone calls they clearly cannot be used for office calls. Most firms do not object to occasional short personal calls being made by members of the firm on the firm's telephone. Likewise, incoming personal calls are generally accepted provided that they are limited in both duration and frequency. It is one thing to take a call to arrange to meet for a drink after work, quite another to gossip for twenty minutes or make a long distance personal call at the firm's expense.'

(Shurman, 1989)
(para 4.2.2)

(2) This type of shorthand concealing a bombshell is universal. On the one hand the bank is better off. On the other hand the lay borrower may regard this as typical lawyer weasliness. Whatever view one takes about that, the disadvantage is that words no longer mean what they say and this is dangerous for everybody except those who pore over these documents all day. Contracts become a private world, a secret code which only the inner mandarins understand. They do not take the reader into account.

(para 4.2.2)

(3) 'Appellant initially contends that Yania's descent from the high embankment into the water and the resulting death were caused 'entirely' by the spoken words and blandishments of Bigan delivered at a distance from Yania. The complainant does not allege that Yania slipped or that he was pushed or that Bigan made any physical impact upon Yania. On the contrary, the only inference deducible from the facts alleged in the complaint is that Bigan, by employment of cajolery and inveiglement, caused such a mental impact on Yania that the latter was deprived of his volitions and freedom of choice and placed under a compulsion to jump into the water. Had Yania been a child of tender years or mentally deficient then it is conceivable that taunting or enticement could constitute actionable negligence if it resulted in harm. However, to contend that such conduct directed to an adult in full possession of all his mental faculties constitutes actionable negligence is not only without precedent but is completely without merit.'

(para 4.3.2)

2   Without re-writing, evaluate whether some of the following sentences should be in a different paragraph. Explain why.

(i)   On March 13, 1963 Maryanne Gerardi sustained serious injury as a result of being run over by her neighbour, John Baseltine. The accident occurred just outside Maryanne's family home. She was then just 23 months old. Maryanne had followed Mr Baseltine out of the house after his visit to celebrate the birthday of Maryanne's mother. He had consumed no alcohol. Mr Baseltine was simply unaware of Maryanne's presence. By the time Mr Baseltine drove off, Maryanne had bent over to pick up her doll which had fallen under the car. Mr Baseltine drove over her and did not discover what had happened until he stopped halfway down the street in response to the screams of Maryanne's mother. Eighteen years later Maryanne still endures the consequences of the accident. Her prognosis suggests that she will still need further plastic surgery to correct scarring on her facing; the pelvic injuries sustained mean that if she can conceive, she will only be able to deliver a child by caesarian section.

(para 4.2.3)

(ii) On March 13, 1963 Maryanne Gerardi sustained serious injury as a result of being run over by her neighbour, John Baseltine. On August 14, 1973 Mr Baseltine's solicitor on his client's behalf admitted liability in a letter. The accident occurred just outside Maryanne's family home. She was then just 23 months old. Maryanne had followed Mr Baseltine out of the house after his visit to celebrate the birthday of Maryanne's mother. He had consumed no alcohol. Mr Baseltine was simply unaware of Maryanne's presence. By the time Mr Baseltine drove off, Maryanne had bent over her and did not discover what had happened until he stopped halfway down the street in response to the screams of Maryanne's mother.

(para 4.2.3)

3   Re-order the sentences in this paragraph in as many ways as you can. Explain the rationale underlying the new order.

Dark green, leafy vegetables such as kale and spinach are good sources of Vitamin C and iron. Carrots, squash and sweet potatoes are good sources of carotene, which the body changes to Vitamin A. All vegetables are good for us because they provide important vitamins and minerals that build cells and keep us healthy. Vitamin C, for example, builds strong teeth and helps us resist infection. Vitamin A keeps skin healthy and protects our eyes. Iron, an important part of vegetables, builds red blood cells

(para 4.2.4)

Managing Sentences

Identify the problems in the following sentences:

(i)   Pursuant to a section 14(1) of the Finance Act requiring a person to lodge a return annually.

(para 5.2.1)

(ii)   It has been decided that the highest amount you are likely to be offered in compensation for the loss of your right arm is considerably less than that which was advised originally.

(para 5.2.1)

(iii)   The form attached should be completed today and returned by courier immediately since it is already overdue for lodgment.

(para 5.2.1)

(iv)   While discussion between aggrieved parties are preferable to instant recourse to the courts, there is something unpalatable about the recent spate of court settlements.

(para 5.2.1)

(v)   None of the arguments are acceptable.

(para 5.2.1)

(vi)   Jonathan is among the few able lawyers who has succeeded in politics.

(para 5.2.1)

(vii)   This is one of the most illogical arguments that has ever been made.

(para 5.2.1)

(viii)   The specific allegations of fraud against the defendant include:

•   falsely stating that the sworn market value of the property was $250,000

•   failing to state that the dishwasher and antique light fittings were not the property of the defendant

•   to represent that the house was authentic Federation period.

(para 5.2.1)

(ix)   The factory is a place where snails and the slimy trails of snails were frequently found.

(para 5.2.1)

(x)   More specifically, lawyers have been accused of failing to sensibly group verbs together and of failing to meticulously keep infinitives together. They have often answered this accusation by resolutely stating that the content requires the peculiar writing style. They have, with the best possible intentions, resisted this advice on Plain English for a long time.

(para 5.2.1)

(xi)   We suggest therefore that the payment which could properly be characterised as an ex gratia payment should attract minimal tax liability unless the Commissioner considers the underlying claim an enforceable contract.

(para 5.2.2)

(xii)   Although a guarantor may give a guarantee to ensure that a customer is granted a particular loan the discharge of the loan does not release the guarantor the personal obligations and collateral given under the guarantee will still apply.

(para 5.2.2)

(xiii)   From the transcript of evidence it is clear that the
bank manager assisted the guarantor to execute the
guarantee validly and then he left the room.

(para 5.2.2)

(xiv)   In these circumstances, it is appropriate for the legal
profession to assert its right to determine the standards of
prospective entrants to the profession by declining to
recognise the adequacy of training offered by institutions
which are inadequately resourced.

(para 5.4.2)

(xv)   The facts as given raise questions about whether
unjust enrichment might apply, what defences might be
open to the purchaser and the remedies which might be
available to you.

(para 5.4.3)

(xvi)   If, contrary to our recommendation, the majority's
view that rights of audience should be extended to
solicitors in the Crown Courts is adopted, we accept that it
is essential that those rights should not be exercised by
any solicitor who had not satisfied an appropriate body that
he was sufficiently skilled for the purpose.

(para 5.5.1)

(xvii)   We immediately sought to uncover the extent of the
wrongdoing and identify the wrongdoers.

(para 5.5.2)

(xviii) When he was seventeen he was expelled from
school in Sydney, and during the next 33 years, he lived a
lusty and full life which was also colourful, if restless.

(para 5.5.2)

(xix)   The responsibility of the parliament is to make laws which are then for the executive to administer and afterwards such laws must be interpreted by the judges.

(para 5.5.2)

(xx)   The lawyer told his secretary to either staple the document or to bind it.

(para 5.5.2)

(xxi)   All trainee solicitors are entitled to both four weeks' holiday and five days' study leave.

(para 5.5.2)

Choosing Words

How and why might you change words used in the following examples?

(i)   We command you to attach [the Defendant], so as to have him before us in our Supreme Court, there to answer us, as well touching a contempt which he it is alleged hath committed against us, as also such other matters as shall be then and there laid to his charge, and further to perform and abide such order as our said court shall make in this behalf; and hereof, fail not, and bring this writ with you.

(para 6.1)

(ii)   For His Excellency's information, I beg to state that the winter season in this place is extremely cold and damp, and trust that the warm clothing for the convicts of this establishment may be furnished as soon as possible, and beg leave to recommend that the shoes should be of a better and more lasting description that what is generally furnished, as we have no means of repairing them.

(para 6.1)

(iii)   A law may be defined as an assemblage of signs declarative of a volition conceived or adopted by the sovereign in a state, concerning the conduct to be observed in a certain case by a certain person or class of persons, who in the case in question are or are supposed to be subject to his power: such volition trusting for its accomplishment to the expectation of certain events which it is intended such declaration should upon occasion be a means of bringing to pass, and the prospect of which it is intended should act as a motive upon those whose conduct is in question.

(para 6.2)

(iv)   Would you be good enough to ...

We should be grateful if you would ...

We would ask that you ...

... is predicated on the assumption that ...

... in connection with ...

... in relation to ...

... in respect of ...

... in the event of ...

... with regard to ...

(para 6.4.3)

(v)   A client should ensure that his business operates on a sound footing.

(para 6.6)

(vi)   This rule applies to each company director who has an independent responsibility to ensure that the company does not trade while insolvent and pledges his assets to creditors accordingly.

(para 6.6)

(vii)   The applicant should complete this form in his handwriting.

(para 6.6)

(viii) Lawyers generally quite like to reinforce their language with adjectives or adverbs that reduce or intensify meaning.

(para 6.7)

(ix)   Our clients are generally concerned about the really serious plight of the defendants in this particular class action.

(para 6.7)

(x)   Obviously our clients are particularly concerned about the apparently serious plight of the defendants in this class.

(para 6.7)

(xi)   Our clients are most concerned about the plight of the defendants in this really critical class action.

(para 6.7)

Turning Advice into Action

What changes would you make to the letter below?
(Please infer the context.)

Dear Sir,

I refer to your meeting with me on March 19.

You instruct that the lessee company rarely paid the rent on time as almost invariably the cheques were dated the 28th or 29th of the month when the due date was the 27th. The tenants also breached the lease by paying insurances required by clauses 7.2 and 7.3 late and failing to send you the certificates.

Furthermore, after a complaint about an electrical fault, your own electrician reported that the cable had been eaten by mice who appear to have been attracted by a kitchen kept in less than wholesome order. During two years of the lease the lessee company failed to pay the local authority taxes. A wall in the kitchen on the second floor was also so affected by the steam rising from the instant water heater which was installed by the lessee company after seeking your consent but was not fitted with the steam outlet in accordance with specifications shown to you, that the damp has now become a structural fault on the north wall of the whole building.

The estate agent managing the lease for you has sent a number of notices directing the tenants to comply with the provisions of the lease, but these have been ignored. You have instructed that legal fees and penalty interest are also now owing in respect of these notices.

Please let me know about any other breaches of the lease. You should feel free to amend or add to any of the breaches listed above. Once the list of breaches has been settled I can proceed to issue the requisite repairs notices and to prepare a letter of demand for the money outstanding.

You also think that the tenant might want to exercise an option to renew or to assign the lease to a third party.

If you have any questions, please do not hesitate to contact me. In the meantime, I look forward to your instructions about any amendments or additions you might have to a list of the breaches by the tenant.

Yours sincerely,

Janet Hazlehurst

Appendix

B Three weeks to better writing

Week One: focus on problem and conclusion

1.1 Is the law right?

1.2 Has the letter begun at the reader's beginning?

1.3 Are the problems to be solved set out preferably in question form?

1.4 Does the conclusion match the statement of the problem without raising more problems?

1.5. Does the recipient know what is to be done next by whom?

Week Two: pattern and patterning

2.1 Does the letter follow a clear overall pattern moving from the general to the particular?

2.2 Are there clear transitions between each of the patterns which are advance organised?

2.3 Are sections and sub-sections patterned appropriately?

Week Three: paragraphs and sentences

3.1 Are there short sentences in introductions, transitions and conclusions with headings used to aid scanning?

3.2 Does each paragraph begin with a topic sentence?

3.3 Do the paragraphs have visual appeal?

Appendix

C The seven step guide to revising

1 The solution and the facts relied upon should be correct

Check for conformity to your instructions and correctness in law.

2 The solution must match the statement of the problem

You should have answered all the questions posed by the client and raised no others which are left unanswered. This also involves a check to see that you have explained basic concepts following the Golden Rule - using language which is consistent, concrete and active.

3 Begin at the reader's beginning

For the introduction, check that you have made a transition for the reader by referring to what the reader knows already and then moving to the issues that you will deal with.

4 Overall patterns and patterns within sections and sub-sections

Is each introduction and transition advance organised? Identify the underlying rationale for patterning of information overall, and in each section and sub-section. Is the underlying rationale - logic (moving from the general to the particular, with conclusions first) time (eg chronology, cause-effect) values (eg most to least recommended, most to least expensive) structure (eg common legal order, following a document).

5   Features of each paragraph

Check whether the paragraph is:

- introductory,
- supporting,
- transitional; or
- concluding.

Check that the paragraph:

- begins with a topic sentence;
- has unity of content;
- has visual appeal;
- if a subordinate structure, moves from the general to the particular;
- if a co-ordinate structure, uses parallel and co-ordinate expressions.

6   Features of each sentence

For each sentence check that it:

- only contains one idea;
- is not ambiguous;
- uses simple, clear, concrete, inclusive, active language;
- mostly is in the order subject + verb + object;
- avoids wordy expressions and archaisms;
- is grammatically correct.

7   Typos and omissions

Read separately for common typographical errors (typos) and typing errors or omissions affecting meaning (Margots). Read the parts you agonised over the most, remembering Bradley's law. (Bradley's law: typos and omissions cluster where there is greatest doubt.)

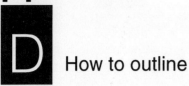

Appendix

D How to outline

How to outline

1 Brainstorm and list

Write in random order a list of the concepts that need to be dealt with and the questions which need to be answered. Settle on the basic vocabulary: how you will refer to the parties, which terms of art need to be used and explained.

2 Problem and recommendation

Write down a problem statement in language which is simple, clear, concrete and active. If you can, write down your conclusions and recommendations next to the problem. You might have to go through the next steps, though, and do this last.

3 Re-order your list

Decide the topics that need to be dealt with from your random list and the ways in which you will sequence the information. Give each section and sub-section a notional heading, whether you intend to use headings in the text or not. Each section and sub-section should contain no more than 7 items. Each sub-section should be capable of being dealt with in fewer than 7 paragraphs.

4 Recommendation

Complete your problem statement by writing your recommendations which you should have had time to conclude at the sub-conscious level through dealing with order. If you noted them at the time of noting the problem, check that they are correct now. You might need to spiral around these steps several times before you have the problem statement, recommendation and topics for discussion in appropriate order. You should not really do a first draft until you have made decisions about these and have decided upon an answer.